The Arden
Shakespeare Miscellany

Jane Armstrong

Arden Shakespeare

1 3 5 7 9 10 8 6 4 2

First published in Great Britain in 2011 by Methuen Drama

Copyright © Jane Armstrong 2011

Arden Shakespeare is an imprint of Methuen Drama

Methuen Drama
A & C Black Publishers Limited
36 Soho Square
London W1D 3QY
www.methuendrama.com
www.ardenshakespeare.com

A CIP catalogue record for this book is available
from the British Library

ISBN 978 1 408 12910 4

Available in the USA from Bloomsbury Academic & Professional,
175 Fifth Avenue / 3rd Floor, New York, NY 10010.
www.BloomsburyAcademicUSA.com

Designed and typeset by Country Setting, Kingsdown, Kent
Printed and bound by Zrinski, Croatia

This book is produced using paper that is made from wood
grown in managed, sustainable forests. It is natural, renewable
and recyclable. The logging and manufacturing processes
conform to the environmental regulations of the country of origin

Contents

Illustrations

Foreword

This book owes a great debt to the Arden Shakespeare and to the many Arden editors I have worked with over the years, especially to Richard Proudfoot, who has been the best of companions along the way, and from whom I have learned so much. Barbara Hodgdon has been a wonderful correspondent and the source of many enjoyable and thought-provoking emails. My thanks, also, to Margaret Bartley, who took the book on and has been marvellously positive and helpful, Anna Brewer, for her help with illustrations, and Simon Trussler, who has done a fine job on the design. Above of all, thanks to Joe, who thought of it.

Quotations from and references to Shakespeare's works are taken from individual volumes in the Arden Shakespeare series or from *The Arden Shakespeare Complete Works*. The Q1 and Q2 versions of Hamlet's 'To be, or not to be' speech on pp. 90–1 are from the Q1- and Q2-based editions by Ann Thompson and Neil Taylor in the Arden Shakespeare series. Grouped stage directions are drawn directly from Folio and Quarto sources (with modernised spelling) though referenced to Arden line-numbering. Other works referred to are listed on pp. 205–7. Details of first recorded performances are given after play synopses where they date from Shakespeare's lifetime.

I

'Speak of Me as I Am'

The Life

Will who?

*The spelling 'Shakespeare' only became fully established
in the twentieth century. Dozens of earlier versions included:*

Shackspere

Shakspere / Shakspeare
(his own spellings)

Shagspere

Shaxpere
(on his marriage licence)

Shaxberd

Shexpere

Shakeshaft
(William, possibly a player, in a Lancashire Catholic household,
identified by some with Shakespeare)

Shakespear
(William Hazlitt, George Bernard Shaw)

Shakspere
(Samuel Taylor Coleridge,
the scholar F. J. Furnivall)

'Shakerags'
(the disgruntled actor Will Kemp, after parting
company with the Chamberlain's Men)

'An upstart crow'
(fellow-writer Robert Greene)

Fig. 1 (opposite). William Shakespeare, the Cobbe Portrait, artist unknown, c. 1610.

Fig. 2 (page 4, top). William Shakespeare, the Chandos Portrait, attrib. John Taylor, oil on canvas, c. 1610.

Fig. 3 (page 4, bottom). William Shakespeare, after Geerhart Janssen, plaster cast of copy of head of effigy at Stratford-upon-Avon, c. 1620.

Fig. 4 (page 5). William Shakespeare, Martin Droeshout, engraving, frontispiece, First Folio, 1623.

What did Shakespeare look like?

Everyone knows what Shakespeare looked like: balding, with an impressive rounded forehead and a ruff. However, there are only three portraits with any possibility of authority, and one of these certainly dates from after his death. The monument to Shakespeare in Holy Trinity church at Stratford-upon-Avon, from about 1620, bears some resemblance to these three but was restored in the eighteenth century. The many other portraits of him are derivatives, false claimants or works of the imagination.

The Cobbe portrait

A painting only recently identified as a possible portrait of Shakespeare has become a front-runner for the preferred representation. It shows a considerably more elegant and gentlemanly figure than we are used to. Long in the possession of the Cobbe family in Ireland, it was spotted as the original from which several copies were made; one of these, in the Folger Shakespeare Library in Washington, was until 70 years ago described as a possible portrait of Shakespeare, while others have been traditionally identified with him since the seventeenth century. The painting dates from before Shakespeare's death, but the family identification of it with the playwright dates from a century later.

The Cobbe family were connected by marriage to Shakespeare's patron, Henry Wriothesley, 3rd Earl of Southampton, and an inscription on the original from Horace, addressed to a playwright, potentially strengthens the case. The Cobbe family are also the owners of a portrait, supposedly of Henry Wriothesley, representing an extremely dandyish young man with long hair and an earring.

The Chandos portrait

The National Portrait Gallery in London holds the only other portrait probably painted in Shakespeare's lifetime. It is usually dated to around 1610, and is attributed to John Taylor, a professional painter, though it has also been suggested as the work of the actor and manager Richard Burbage, himself a competent artist. It is named after a former owner, the 1st Duke of Chandos, and in 1856 became the founding picture in the National Portrait Gallery,

where it is numbered NPG1. It shows a man of generally similar appearance to the more familiar First Folio engraving opposite, though thinner of face and with an alert, though contained, expression quite different from the wooden Droeshout version. His dress and general appearance are far more informal than those of the Cobbe portrait, and he sports an earring in his left ear which is original, though the beard and hair were probably lengthened at a later date.

The Janssen bust

A memorial bust attributed to Geerhart Janssen (of Dutch origin) was put up in Holy Trinity church in Stratford-upon-Avon around four years after Shakespeare's death, presumably at the behest and with the approval of his family. Opinion differs as to how much it may have been altered by its restoration around 1748. The disappointingly portly figure may simply reflect Shakespeare's appearance at the very end of his life.

The Droeshout engraving

This Shakespeare has no beard. The frontispiece of the First Folio (1623) carries the well-known portrait engraved by Martin Droeshout (either a Flemish Protestant refugee, or his son of the same name). It was no doubt commissioned by the friends who organised the publication, and is mentioned by Ben Jonson in his dedication *To the Reader*, which perhaps politely suggests a close likeness:

> This Figure, that thou here seest put,
>   It was for gentle Shakespeare cut;
> Wherein the Graver had a strife
>   With Nature, to out-do the life:
> O, could he but have drawn his wit
>   As well in brass, as he hath hit
> His face . . .

The £20 note

From 1970 to 1991 Shakespeare featured on the Bank of England's £20 note, designed by Harry Eccleston. This much reproduced image was taken from Shakespeare's statue in Poets' Corner, Westminster Abbey (designed by William Kent and made by Peter Scheemakers in 1740).

What was he like?

I loved the man, and do honour his memory
— on this side Idolatry — as much as any.
Ben Jonson

Ben Jonson reports that Shakespeare was 'indeed honest, and of an open and free nature', which seems to have been a general opinion. The printer and playwright Henry Chettle, who had been involved in the publication of Robert Greene's scathing and envious remarks about an 'upstart crow' (and may indeed even have written them himself), wrote apologetically that various respectable persons had 'reported his uprightness of dealing, which argues his honesty, and his facetious grace in writing, that approves his art'. Shakespeare was reputed to be 'gentle', and good company, but determined about his work – he would refuse an invitation to the tavern in favour of writing, not least, perhaps, because most of the daytime would have been taken up by theatre business, rehearsal and performance. He was no slouch at a lawsuit, and energetic in professional and business affairs. He was alone among his contemporaries in combining the roles of playwright, theatre 'sharer', or joint manager, and actor. Later writers had no hesitation in divining the character of the man.

He was the man of all Modern, and perhaps Ancient Poets,
with the largest and most comprehensive soul.
John Dryden, 1668

Our myriad-minded Shakespeare.
Samuel Taylor Coleridge, 1817

Was Shakespeare a Catholic?

In 1534, under the Act of Supremacy, Henry VIII (1491–1547) finally declared himself head of the Church in England. However, the split from Rome was politically and financially inspired rather than doctrinal, and he remained essentially Catholic in his beliefs, and antagonistic to Protestant doctrine. After his death, the ascendancy of the Protestant party led to bitter division, and under Thomas Cranmer, adviser to Henry's son, Edward VI, the Church became virulently Protestant. Measures to restore Catholicism during the brief reign of Mary and her Spanish husband Philip were reversed under the Protestant Elizabeth. Her successor James, son of the Catholic Mary, Queen of Scots, was also officially a Protestant, and a firm believer in the divine right of kings. During the reigns of both Elizabeth and James, fear of Catholic plots led to widespread and sometimes draconian persecution of Catholics.

Under Protestant rulings, penalties were imposed for failure to attend church under the new dispensation, and many saints' days were removed from the calendar and customary parish practices forbidden. Everyday life in towns and villages was greatly changed. Shakespeare's parents were of a generation born and brought up in a Catholic world (his father, John, was born sometime in the 1520s; his mother's birth date is unknown); William himself was born after the accession of Elizabeth. A number of pieces of evidence attest to the continuing Catholic sympathies of members of both the Shakespeare and Arden families, but there is no specific reason to assume that William shared what may have been the religious views of other members of his family. All we can safely say is that whatever his views were, he kept them to himself.

> *I never felt so strongly as now that language*
> *was given to me to conceal rather than to reveal —*
> *I have no words at all to say what is in my heart.*
>
> Ellen Terry

FOR	AGAINST

Family

Shakespeare's father was probably the John Shakespeare listed amongst Warwickshire recusants (those who failed to take Holy Communion) in 1592.*

Edward Arden, a connection of his mother, was hanged in 1583, convicted of conspiracy to murder Queen Elizabeth.

There was strong Catholic representation in the area round Stratford-upon-Avon.

In 1606 Shakespeare's daughter Susanna was fined for recusancy. She rather swiftly married a staunch Protestant.

Life

Some scholars have argued that the 'lost' (i.e. undocumented) years between Shakespeare's youth in Stratford and his arrival on the theatrical scene were spent in a private house in Lancashire, where one William Shakeshaft is recorded in a document of 1581 relating to players and properties belonging to the Catholic Alexander Houghton, of Lea Hall. Shakeshaft was, though, a common name in Lancashire.

Works

Some have found embedded references to Catholic issues and specific events in many of the plays. In *As You Like It*, for example, the exiled aristocrats in the Forest of Arden (an imaginary place recalling Shakespeare's Warwickshire but also the Ardennes) could have called to mind Catholics exiled in northern Europe.

Family

The simple documentary evidence of his baptism, marriage and will indicates an outwardly straightforward Anglican history. Anything else, though, would be unlikely, as any suggestion of Catholic sympathies in the wording of such documents and of bequests would be risky.

Life

Lived for at least six years in the house of a French Huguenot refugee in London.

Works

Many would argue that there is no direct evidence for Catholic sympathies in the plays, and that they are secular in tone. They are generally warmly sympathetic to his characters' religious beliefs, and

Some references to the Bible may be taken from the Catholic Rheims version.

The plays reveal an interest in issues where doctrinal differences affect politics, particularly questions of the legitimacy and divine right of kings. These were, however, subjects under general (if cautious) debate at the time.

There is nostalgia for happier times when the celebration of holy days and popular festivals was part of the fabric of everyday life; and also for the monasteries and abbeys so recently destroyed, and now 'Bare ruined choirs' (Sonnet 73). This may or may not indicate Catholic sympathies.

* *It was long thought that a 'spiritual will' found in the mid-eighteenth century by a tiler working on the roof of the Shakespeare family house in Henley Street, and claimed as John Shakespeare's, was proof of his abiding Catholic faith. This document has recently been discredited.*

to romance religious figures such as friars. Sympathy is not extended, however, to cardinals and popes, nor to two Puritan figures: Malvolio (*Twelfth Night*), a humourless killjoy, is made fun of and brought low, socially excommunicated, as it were; the icy Angelo (*Measure for Measure*) is excoriated for his hypocrisy.

The plays show deep familiarity with the Protestant Geneva Bible of 1560 and other Protestant versions.

Was Shakespeare a lawyer?

The eighteenth-century scholar Edmond Malone suggested that before becoming an actor Shakespeare might have spent some time as a lawyer's clerk, and many have since agreed with him. The plays contain a good deal of legal terminology and reference to law; and, inevitably, most of the surviving documentation relating directly to Shakespeare's life consists of everyday legal records. He seems to have been mildly litigious, and was involved in a number of minor lawsuits. In his plays he may simply, however, have been catering to the interests of his audiences – which often included lawyers from the Inns of Court – and enjoying the language.

Was Shakespeare bisexual?

Shakespeare was, of course, a married man and the father of several children. He clearly spent most of his time from the early 1590s away from home; and, notoriously, all he specifically bequeathed his wife was their second best bed (opinion differs as to whether or not this indicates an unhappy relationship). He was also the subject of anecdotes about extramarital heterosexual activity, and many of the sonnets are addressed to a woman with whom the poet seems to have a sexual relationship. The first group of sonnets, addressed to and in praise of a young man, has, however, given rise to enduring speculation that Shakespeare was gay, or at least bisexual. The latter seems most likely.

Admiration and love for the young man of the sonnets is lavishly expressed, though as he is the addressee some of this is to be expected. However, the overtly sexual, as opposed to idealised and spiritual, relationship of the sonnets is with the woman addressed in the later poems, rather than with the man. The key text is Sonnet 20, where the young man is described as having 'A woman's face with nature's own hand painted', and as 'the master mistress of my passion'. It concludes, though, that in making him, Nature added 'one thing to my purpose nothing', and 'pricked thee out for women's pleasure'. 'Mine be thy love, and thy love's use their treasure' – the ending is written to suggest a platonic love. The intensity of the relationship with the young man in the sonnets has historically caused dismay and anguish to some admirers of Shakespeare, as well as enthusing gay/queer readers, Oscar Wilde among them.

There are hints of homosexuality in some of the plays, and in some of the roles given to boy players. Antonio's apartness and melancholy in *The Merchant of Venice*, and his willingness to risk everything for Bassanio, have been successfully represented as deriving from his homosexuality, and Hamlet's melancholy and alienation, along with his reliance on Horatio as his only friend, have been ascribed to the same cause. Shakespeare, of course, was able to portray many different approaches to life without embodying all of them himself.

ALL'S WELL THAT ENDS WELL

c. 1602–5

This 'problem play', whose conclusion, like that of its darker near contemporary *Measure for Measure*, depends on a 'bed trick', unsettlingly combines elements of folktale with sometimes uncomfortable realism. Like *Measure for Measure*, its 'happy' ending raises more questions than it answers.

Helena, a physician's daughter, loves above her station, but is awarded the hand of Bertram, the man she loves, by the King of France, whom she has healed from sickness. The reluctant Bertram vows to consummate the marriage only if she can give him his own ring and a child to whom he is father – apparently an impossibility – and goes off to the wars. With the help of Diana, a young woman whom Bertram is attempting to seduce, Helena obtains the ring and, in disguise, conceives his child. Helena's death is reported, and Bertram attempts to marry a third woman. He offers her a ring given him by the disguised Helena, and the truth comes to light. Helena, now pregnant, reappears, and Bertram is obliged to fulfil his vow. Faithlessness is also explored in the character of Bertram's braggart friend Parolles, and it is chiefly the older generation, especially the Countess of Rossillion, the King and the old lord Lafew, who show wisdom and generosity.

Peggy Ashcroft was a memorable Countess in Trevor Nunn's 1981 production for the Royal Shakespeare Company. When a letter from Bertram arrived, she clearly knew what was in it, and put off reading it. She put the letter on a little table by her chair. Then she reached into her pocket for her glasses and carefully put them on, then even more carefully broke the seal on the letter and slowly opened it. As she read, her whole upper body sagged, but only briefly.

The grey cardigan she wore was worn by Alexandra Gilbreath both as Paulina in *The Winter's Tale* and as Katherina in *The Taming of the Shrew*. The cardigan came to be called 'The Peggy'.

Did writing come easily to Shakespeare?

There are two different versions of Shakespeare's compositional habits. John Heminges and Henry Condell declare in their introductory address to the First Folio that 'we have scarce received from him a blot in his papers'. His fellow-playwright Ben Jonson noted that this claim was often made by the players 'as an honour to Shakespeare', but that in thinking it a compliment they were mistaken. He seems to believe the description valid up to a point – Shakespeare 'had an excellent Fancy, brave notions and gentle expressions, wherein he flowed with that facility that sometimes it was necessary he should be stopped'. The introductory verses to the First Folio, however, suggest a more complex, and surely convincing, picture:

> For though the Poet's matter, Nature be,
>   His Art doth give the fashion. And, that he,
> Who casts to write a living line, must sweat,
>   (Such as thine are) and strike the second heat
> Upon the Muses' anvil: turn the same,
>   (And himself with it) that he thinks to frame;
> Or for the laurel, he may gain a scorn,
>   For a good Poet's made, as well as born.
> And such wert thou.

'The Book of Sir Thomas More', a play manuscript by a number of authors, contains sections which are very probably by Shakespeare, the longest of them a passage of 165 lines which includes a powerful speech to the crowd by More. This manuscript shows some evidence of rethinking in the course of composition. It is written clearly in a practised and elegant hand (see p. 96).

Shakespeare himself, as James Shapiro points out, describes Lucrece sitting down to write in lines which have the ring of personal experience (and perhaps a hint of it in the use of the word 'will'):

> What wit sets down is blotted straight with will.
> This is too curious-good; this blunt and ill.
>   Much like a press of people at a door
>   Throng her inventions which shall go before.
>   (*The Rape of Lucrece* 1299–1302)

[12]

Did Shakespeare contribute to the King James Bible?

It has been persistently suggested that Shakespeare was on the distin-guished editorial team involved in the preparation of the King James Bible (the Authorised Version), published in 1611. All serious scholars reject the idea, and its attendant 'proof' – the discovery that in Psalm 46, the 46th word from the beginning is 'shake' and the 46th from the end 'spear', proposed as a hidden reference to the fact that in the year before publication Shakespeare would have been 46 years old. Several other translations contain the same 'clue', some of them predating Shake-speare's birth.

Shakespeare on stage

Shakespeare probably began his theatrical career as an actor. His name appears in cast lists of the Chamberlain's Men, though without the assignation of any particular role. He was named in 1598 as one of the 'principal comedians' in Ben Jonson's *Every Man in his Humour*, and in 1603 as one of the 'principal tragedians' in Jonson's *Sejanus*, so he was evidently up to major roles, and versatile.

It has been suggested that he played the Chorus in *Henry V*, and tradition has it that he played old men – the countryman Adam in *As You Like It*, the ghost of Hamlet's father, King Henry in the *Henry IV* plays and Duncan in *Macbeth*. Nicholas Rowe, in the first biography of Shakespeare, noted (disparagingly) that his role as the Ghost in *Hamlet* was seen as 'the top of his performance'.

Parents and siblings

John Shakespeare (1520s–1601), born in Snitterfield near Stratford-upon-Avon, married Mary Arden (d. 1608), a farmer's daughter and one of eight children, somewhere around 1557. (It was only established in 2002 that the farm near Stratford long described as Mary Arden's House had no connection with the family, and that Mary Arden's childhood home was in fact the house next door.) John was a glover and whittawer. A whittawer bought animal skins from butchers and prepared them for glove-making; calf-killing recurs as a 'murder' theme through Shakespeare's plays, notably in *Julius Caesar* and *Hamlet*, perhaps as a result of the young William's early experiences.

John Shakespeare initially prospered, and became a Stratford citizen of some standing, serving on the town council and in a number of senior positions including alderman, bailiff and justice of the peace. At the same time, however, he was being prosecuted for offences of usury and illegal dealing in wool. From the mid-1570s he began to suffer financial troubles, mortgaging or losing much of his property, including land that Mary had brought with her to the marriage, and there are records of disorderly behaviour. The family lived through some years of uncertainty, and it is likely that William's education was curtailed.

In 1592 John was listed as a recusant, and as failing to go to church for fear of prosecution for debt. Thereafter, however, matters improved. In 1596, when with William's input he was granted a coat of arms, he was recorded as being once again a substantial landowner. Perhaps his son's success had helped him out of difficulty.

William was the third of eight children born to John and Mary Shakespeare – the first to survive infancy, and the first boy. He was, in practical terms, an eldest child, and may well have been treasured by his mother. Three girls, Joan, Margaret and Anne, died in early childhood. A second Joan, born eleven years after the first, married successfully, lived to 1646, and seems to have remained on good terms with her brother. Apart from William she was the only member of the family to produce surviving children. There were three younger brothers.

The youngest, Edmund, followed his brother to London to become an actor, and died in the cold winter of 1607, in the same year as his infant son Edward. Gilbert, a haberdasher, having taken up a similar profession to that of his father, also spent some time in London. Nothing is known of Richard.

In her 1928 lectures *A Room of One's Own*, Virginia Woolf speculated about an imaginary sister, Judith – a gifted and intelligent woman denied the opportunity to develop her abilities by the mores of her day. She writes in secret, is beaten by her father when she refuses to marry, and runs away to a sad end in pregnancy and suicide.

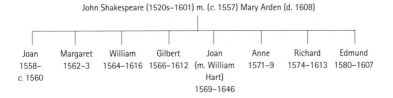

John Shakespeare (1520s–1601) m. (c. 1557) Mary Arden (d. 1608)

Joan	Margaret	William	Gilbert	Joan	Anne	Richard	Edmund
1558–	1562–3	1564–1616	1566–1612	(m. William	1571–9	1574–1613	1580–1607
c. 1560				Hart)			
				1569–1646			

Parents and children

Richard responds to his mother's tirade:

DUCHESS   I prithee, hear me speak.
KING RICHARD
  You speak too bitterly.
DUCHESS   Hear me a word,
  For I shall never speak to thee again.
KING RICHARD So.

                              Richard III 4.4.180–3

Katherina flounces out:

KATHERINA
  Why, and I trust I may go too, may I not?
  What, shall I be appointed hours, as though, belike,
  I knew not what to take and what to leave? Ha!   *Exit.*

                The Taming of the Shrew 1.1.102–4

Shakespeare's children

'Witty above her sex, but that's not all,
Wise to salvation was good Mistress Hall.'

William married Anne Hathaway (*c.* 1555–1623), a local girl nearly
ten years older than himself, in November 1582. They had three
children, all born within a few years of their parents' marriage.
Susanna was baptised in May 1583, so Anne was pregnant at the time
of the marriage; Hamnet and Judith, twins, were born in 1585.

Susanna

Susanna married the Protestant Dr John Hall in 1607 – perhaps a
wise move after having been reported, with twenty other Stratford
citizens, for refusing to take communion at Easter the previous year,
which suggests Catholic sympathies. Her father made a generous
marriage settlement, and at his death left her and her husband most of
his property. Legal documents indicate that she could read and write.
She died in 1649, and her gravestone is inscribed with an appreciative
poem whose first lines appear above.

Judith

Judith married late, at the age of 31, and in difficult circumstances.
She and her intended, Thomas Quiney, who was her junior by four
years, did not obtain the special licence necessary for marrying in Lent.
When they were summoned before the consistory court Quiney failed
to appear, and was excommunicated. The urgency of the marriage
may have been caused by a separate scandal. In the month following the
marriage, Quiney was accused of immorality with a young woman
who had recently been buried with her child, probably after dying in
childbirth. He pleaded guilty, and was sentenced to pay public pen-
ance in church. On his offering to pay a 5*s*. fine, to go to the poor, this
was reduced to making a formal apology. He was obviously an
unsatisfactory son-in-law, and Shakespeare altered his will to protect

his daughter's interests. The marriage lasted, however, and the couple had three children. Judith died in 1662.

Hamnet

Susanna's twin and the Shakespeares' only son, Hamnet, died at the age of eleven. The twins must have been named after Shakespeare's friends Hamnet and Judith Sadler, who may well have been their god-parents. Hamnet Sadler – his name was sometimes spelled Hamlet (the two spellings were interchangeable variants) – was a Stratford baker, and a close enough friend to witness Shakespeare's will. The name was quite common at the time.

The father and children cannot have seen much of each other, but the intense and moving father–daughter relationships (more than once involving a long-lost daughter) in Shakespeare's later plays suggest that he might have had strong feelings for them. The quality of Viola's melancholy (*Twelfth Night*) when she believes her twin, Sebastian, has been drowned at sea, is also memorable. The loss of Hamnet may perhaps be felt in Macbeth's regret at his childlessness, the painful death of Lady Macduff's boy (*Macbeth*), and in Constance's moving lament for her son Arthur in *King John* (3.3.93–105).

And William?

The successful poet and playwright William Davenant was reputed to be an illegitimate son of Shakespeare (see p. 21).

The King's Free Grammar School

No Greek but a good deal of Latin

By virtue of his father's position as an alderman of Stratford-upon-Avon, young William was eligible to attend the grammar school and to receive an education which would serve him extremely well as a playwright.

The school probably had fewer than fifty pupils, all boys, whom it took from the age of seven. The curriculum would have been similar to that provided in grammar schools throughout the country, and Shakespeare would have studied something like the following:

A sixteenth-century school curriculum

AT THE INTRODUCTORY LEVEL

The Catechism

Learning psalms by heart

Christiani hominis institutum, by the sixteenth-century humanist scholar Desiderius Erasmus

Introductory Latin grammar, using short extracts from the classics

Collections of *sententiae*, short maxims from classical writers

The study of rhetoric, particularly using Erasmus' *De ... copia*, which provided models for composition and practice in the arts of rhetoric and embellishment

Erasmus' *Colloquies*, short dialogues providing training in speaking Latin

Aesop's fables in Latin

UP TO THE AGE OF TWELVE

Classical comedies by Terence and Plautus

Latin grammar, translation and composition (imitation of classical writers, and essays upon set themes, perhaps taken from Erasmus' *Adagia* (*Adages*)

AT THE HIGHER LEVEL

Latin was spoken at all times

Study of the works of Caesar, Horace, Ovid, Sallust, Virgil and others

Study of the rhetoricians Cicero and Quintilian

The writing of orations and more advanced rhetorical compositions

Boys left school at about sixteen years of age, going to apprenticeships, to university at Oxford or Cambridge (this did not apply to Shakespeare), or perhaps to the Inns of Court to train for the law. Shakespeare may well not have completed his education, as his father's affairs were troubled at the time.

Shakespeare would have left school competent in Latin to a level that may have been scoffed at by his contemporaries (it was Ben Jonson who patronisingly remarked that he had 'small Latin and less Greek'), but that to the average person now would be extremely impressive.

Rhetoric 1

A good grammar-school education gave Shakespeare not only plenty of writing practice, but also a useful working familiarity with rhetorical techniques, and with their purposes as well as with their forms. His deployment of them would have been noted and appreciated by the educated members of his audience, but they are very effective for any listener – even for modern audiences unschooled in their uses and unaccustomed to spotting them.

Rhetorical devices were highly valued by Elizabethan poets, and they can be found in practically every line of Shakespeare's work. In earlier plays – *Richard III* and *Richard II*, *A Midsummer Night's Dream*, *Love's Labour's Lost* and *Romeo and Juliet* – they are very openly on display. In later works they are absorbed more integrally into the flow of speech.

The 'lost years'

The years between Shakespeare's leaving school (date unknown) and Robert Greene's allusion to him in 1592 as a rising star in London are sparsely documented. The gap is punctuated by his marriage in 1582 and the births of his children in 1583 and 1585. Various suggestions have been made as to how he may have earned his living and supported his family during this period, and some of the conjectures are listed overleaf. Clearly, by the time he arrived in London he had decided that he wanted to earn money as a poet, and perhaps also as a playwright: his first published works are poems, but early plays may not have been immediately printed, or printed copies may be lost.

What was he up to?

Butcher's apprentice
according to John Dowdall, a seventeenth-century lawyer

Lawyer's clerk
according to the scholar – and former barrister – Edmond Malone

Country schoolmaster
related by the antiquarian John Aubrey, on fairly good authority:
the story came from William Beeston, an actor whose father
Christopher was an actor in Shakespeare's company

One of the above and occasional nappy-changer
his biographer Katherine Duncan-Jones suggests that he would
have been unlikely to absent himself from home at a time when
he had financial and perhaps practical responsibility for
three small children

Schoolmaster/actor
in the household of Lancashire Catholic landowner
Alexander Houghton, and perhaps later a player with one
of the travelling companies

Soldier
suggested by one William J. Thoms in 1865, and argued
by Duff Cooper in his book *Sergeant Shakespeare* (1949).
Shakespeare might have volunteered or been drafted during
the Armada crisis of 1588, and the plays show familiarity
with soldiers' lives and recruitment practices

Member of Drake's crew
circumnavigating the world on the *Golden Hind*,
proposed by E.V. Everitt in 1954

Shakespeare on the road

At a time when many people did not travel much, Shakespeare, first probably as a travelling player and later making annual visits to Stratford (according to the seventeenth-century antiquary John Aubrey, he 'was wont to goe to his native Countrey once a yeare') did more travelling than most. There is no certain evidence that he went further afield, at least in his adult life, than the English south-east and midlands – though he may well have travelled more widely as a player, and some have argued that he went north or even abroad in his youth. In 1611 he put his name to a list of supporters of a parliamentary bill 'for the better repair of highways'. Gratiano in *The Merchant of Venice* complains about unnecessary roadworks (5.1.263–4).

He regularly broke his journeys to and from home in Oxford. According to Aubrey he stayed at the Crown Inn on the Stratford road, owned by a couple called Davenant, and was later reputed to be the father of young William Davenant, born in 1606. William became a successful playwright and poet laureate, and adapted Shakespeare's plays. He also introduced the practice of engaging women actors to play women's parts later in the seventeenth century. Aubrey reported that 'he writ with the very spirit' of Shakespeare, and seemed happy enough to be thought his son.

Shakespeare's grasp of wider geography was uncertain. Italian towns are wrongly located, and two major errors in *The Winter's Tale* give Bohemia a sea coast and (confusing Delphi with Delos) situate Delphi on an island – the latter an error shared with Robert Greene and others.

Shakespeare the deerstealer

Nicholas Rowe, in his edition of the *Works*, published in 1709, offered a few tales of Shakespeare's life, including one about him being caught taking game from the park of Sir Thomas Lucy, the local landowner, and having to leave Stratford under threat of prosecution.

What his contemporaries thought of him

'Thou Star of Poets'

Shakespeare was very greatly admired by his contemporaries. The number and nature of references to him make the claims of the various authorship doubters unconvincing.

The first surviving reference to his literary and theatrical career appeared in 1592, and was inspired by envy. *Greene's Groats-worth of Wit*, a work compiled from papers of the recently deceased writer Robert Greene, criticised the upstart, bombastic Shakespeare (it refers in passing to a line in *3 Henry VI* (1.4.137), 'O, tiger's heart wrapped in a woman's hide'):

> . . . there is an upstart Crow, beautified with our feathers, that
> with his *Tiger's heart wrapped in a Player's hide*, supposes he is
> as well able to bombast out a blank verse as the best of you;
> and, being an absolute *Johannes fac totum*, is in his own conceit
> the only Shake-scene in a country.

By the end of the century, however, he was already hugely popular and widely quoted, and there are numerous references to his exceptional ability and popularity. John Marston, for example, in his satire *The Scourge of Villainy* (1598), noted the fashion among young gentlemen for imitating Shakespeare's lovers' language:

> I set thy lips abroach, from whence doth flow
> Naught but pure Juliet and Romeo.

In a pair of Cambridge University plays from the turn of the century, *The Return from Parnassus*, one of the characters is given the opening of *Richard III* as an audition piece, and Shakespeare is clearly all the fashion.

From 1598 his name began to appear on the title-pages of the printed quartos of his plays. Putting his name on a publication – however much or little he had had to do with it – was guaranteed to increase sales, and with little formal copyright protection enterprising printer/publishers did just this, causing tangles for scholars to unpick over succeeding centuries.

Poets were more decorous. Edmund Spenser is thought to have referred to Shakespeare as 'A gentler shepherd . . . Whose muse full of high thoughts invention, / Doth like himself heroically sound' in 'Colin Clout's Come Home Again'. His colleague and fellow-playwright Ben Jonson admired him 'on this side Idolatry'. His enco-mium in the introductory matter to the First Folio is headed:

To the memory of my beloved,
The AUTHOR

MR. WILLIAM SHAKESPEARE:
AND

what he hath left us.

Heminges and Condell refer to him in their introduction to the First Folio as 'our Shakespeare', and Jonson in his introductory poem as 'my Shakespeare', 'Sweet Swan of Avon'. Jonson writes:

> Thou art a Monument, without a tomb,
> And art alive still, while thy book doth live

and his verses also include the famous line:

> He was not of an age, but for all time!

All this is appropriate for a commemorative publication. During Shakespeare's lifetime, however, Jonson was much rougher and more critical, though generally good-humouredly so. He pointed out, for instance, that the 'sea coast of Bohemia' specified as a location in *The Winter's Tale* was an impossibility, since Bohemia is landlocked. And he may have been referring to Shakespeare's aspirations to gentility in acquiring a coat of arms when he provided a country bumpkin desiring to be a gentleman with the motto 'Not without mustard' – Shakespeare in similar circumstances had chosen 'Non sanz droict', or 'Not without right'. Although Jonson claimed in conversation that Shakespeare 'wanted Art', his First Folio verses seem to apologise for this, and praise his art as well as his natural gifts.

Retirement

Towards the end of The Tempest, *Shakespeare's last sole-authored play, Prospero renounces his magic. His final speeches are often taken as the playwright's farewell to the theatre.*

> this rough magic
> I here abjure; and when I have required
> Some heavenly music . . .
> I'll break my staff,
> Bury it certain fathoms in the earth,
> And deeper than did ever plummet sound
> I'll drown my book.
>
> (5.1.50–7)

> Now my charms are all o'erthrown,
> And what strength I have's mine own,
> Which is most faint . . .
> But release me from my bands
> With the help of your good hands.
> Gentle breath of yours my sails
> Must fill, or else my project fails,
> Which was to please. Now I want
> Spirits to enforce, art to enchant;
> And my ending is despair,
> Unless I be relieved by prayer,
> Which pierces so that it assaults
> Mercy itself, and frees all faults.
> As you from crimes would pardoned be,
> Let your indulgence set me free.
>
> (Epilogue)

Shakespeare's views of others

Other writers were freer with their references to Shakespeare than he was with reference to them. His tributes tend to be indirect – in the use of words or phrases recalling others' glories. Edmund Spenser's *Faerie Queene* may perhaps be remembered in the mention of 'fairest wights', 'ladies dead, and lovely knights' in Sonnet 106. Shakespeare makes direct quotation from one man only – Christopher Marlowe (see pp. 114–15).

ANTONY AND CLEOPATRA

c. 1606

Following the death of Julius Caesar, the Roman empire is ruled by a triumvirate. But Mark Antony, Octavius Caesar and Lepidus are fighting not only common enemies but among themselves. Antony has been idling in Alexandria with Cleopatra, Queen of Egypt, but after the death of his wife he is persuaded to patch up political alliances by marrying Caesar's sister, Octavia. In Rome, his follower Enobarbus describes the exotic splendour of Cleopatra in her barge. Antony is drawn back to Egypt, where he and Cleopatra prepare for war. After their defeat in the sea battle of Actium, Antony kills himself by falling on his sword, and is carried, dying, to Cleopatra. Cleopatra, fearing that she will be paraded in triumph by the victorious Caesar, sets an asp to her breast and dies, with her companions Iras and Charmian.

Long but fast-moving, the play is written in many short scenes, and is fluid in both structure and language. It oscillates between the sensuality and hedonism of Alexandria and stern, political and pragmatic Rome, coming down on the side of neither but leaving no doubt as to where the poetry lies. For an example of Shakespeare's poetic transformation of his sources, see p. 121.

Shakespeare's will

Shakespeare made his will in early 1616. Notoriously, his sole bequest to his wife was the 'second best bed with the furniture' – and this was in an addendum. Along with the fact that there is no mention in the will of any member of Anne's family, and his making sure that she would not have a claim to his London property, this has been taken to indicate possible coolness between husband and wife.

The main bequests were:

- £100, and interest on an additional £150, along with other smaller items, to his daughter Judith, who was about to marry at the time that the will was made, in 1616

- His Stratford property – his own house New Hall, two houses in Henley Street and various other buildings and pieces of land – to his daughter Susanna; the residue after other bequests also went to Susanna and her husband John Hall

- £20, his 'wearing apparel', and a lifetime tenancy at a small rent of the house she was living in, to his sister Joan Hart

- £5 to each of Joan's three sons

- His plate – a valuable bequest – to his eight-year-old grand-daughter Elizabeth Hall

- £10 to the poor of Stratford

- 26s. 8d. to five men, among them his colleagues Richard Burbage, John Heminges and Henry Condell, to buy rings

No bequest was made to William Davenant of Oxford.

Confusing identities: two doubles

Strangely, there are two characters called Jaques and two called Oliver in *As You Like It*.

- Jaques, the third son of Sir Rowland de Boys
- Jaques, a melancholic lord attending the banished Duke Senior

- Oliver, the eldest son of Sir Rowland de Boys
- Sir Oliver Mar-text, a country priest

What did he die of?

Shakespeare died in Stratford-upon-Avon on 23 April 1616. Tradition has it that this followed a heavy drinking session with the poet Michael Drayton and his old friend and fellow-playwright and poet Ben Jonson. His death at what now seems the early age of 52 should be seen in the context of the rest of his family. He outlived all but one of the four of his siblings who survived infancy.

Lines inscribed on
Shakespeare's commemorative stone
possibly composed by himself

Good friend, for Jesus' sake forbear
To dig the dust enclosed here.
Blest be the man that spares these stones,
And curst be he that moves my bones.

Characters called William

Shakespeare gave two of his characters the same name as himself:

William the country bumpkin in *As You Like It* is slow. Perhaps ironically, given that he shares his name with his creator, his longest sentence is 'Ay sir, I have a pretty wit!' We are told that he was born in the Forest of Arden – William Shakespeare's mother, a Warwickshire girl, was Mary Arden.

William Page, a schoolboy in *The Merry Wives of Windsor*, is catechised on his Latin studies by Sir Hugh Evans in a sequence of questions of the kind that Shakespeare must have been drilled in during his grammar-school days. A Welsh schoolmaster, Thomas Jenkins, was employed at the grammar school at Stratford-upon-Avon.

❧ *Saints* ❧

References to saints are not frequent in Shakespeare's work, but tend to occur in clusters in appropriate places. Most common, appearing in the history plays, are those to the national patron saints George, Denis and David.

Top ten saints

in order of frequency of invocation

GEORGE

CRISPIN and CRISPINIAN

DENIS

PAUL

DAVID

CUPID

ANNE

FRANCIS

NICHOLAS

PETER

also mentioned

BENNET, JAQUES OR JAMES, LAMBERT, LUKE, MARTIN, MICHAEL, PATRICK, STEPHEN, VALENTINE AND THE VIRGIN MARY

'By *St Anne*' was a common oath, but Anne, mother of the Virgin Mary, was particularly disliked by the anti-Marian Puritans; Feste invokes her in affirmation of Sir Toby Belch's anti-Puritan remark: 'Dost thou think because thou art virtuous, there shall be no more cakes and ale?' – 'Yes, by Saint Anne, and ginger shall be hot i'th' mouth, too' (*Twelfth Night* 2.3.113–16). Sly the Warwickshire tinker, indolent onstage audience to *The Taming of the Shrew*, swears by her that he has not nodded off during the entertainment.

In *Measure for Measure* the pious Isabella desires to enter the order of nuns devoted to **St Clare**, virgin contemplative and founder of the Poor Clares under the inspiration of St Francis. (Clare is now the patron saint of television.)

25 October 1415 was the date of the battle of Agincourt, and the day is dedicated to **Crispin** and **Crispinian**, two martyrs who without Shakespeare would have remained even more obscure than they otherwise are. According to legend they were Roman shoemakers who escaped persecution and fled to Kent, where they set up shop in Faversham, in Preston Street. This English connection may make a little more sense of Henry V's six mentions of them on the eve of battle (4.3). 'Crispian' is an alternative version of 'Crispinian' rather than of Crispin.

Cupid, Roman god of love and son of Venus, is called on as a saint, in light-hearted and somewhat worldly fashion, by the Princess of France and by the King of Navarre in *Love's Labour's Lost*, a play about the battle of the sexes.

St David, sixth-century monk and bishop, and patron saint of Wales, appears three times in *Henry V*, home to Shakespeare's 'stage' Welshman Fluellen. 'I do believe your majesty takes no scorn to wear the leek upon Saint Tavy's Day', says Fluellen to Henry, who replies that he wears it 'for a memorable honour, / For I am Welsh, you know, good countryman' (4.7.100-4)

St Denis, Bishop of Paris and patron saint of France, is aptly invoked twice by Charles of France in *1 Henry VI*, and also by Henry V of England – 'Saint Denis be my speed!' – in his somewhat desperate attempt to woo Katherine in poor French (5.2.182-3). He is also called on, slightly extravagantly, with Saint Cupid, by the Princess of France in *Love's Labour's Lost* (5.2.87).

St Francis is invoked twice by Friar Laurence in *Romeo and Juliet*, presumably to indicate that he is a member of the Franciscan order.

Shakespeare's date of birth was perhaps 23 April, *St George*'s Day, or a day or so before. He may have felt particular attachment to the saint for this reason, and also because St George was a high-profile figure in Stratford-upon-Avon, where Holy Trinity church contained an altar dedicated to him and a painting depicting his defeat of the dragon. Over many years Stratford, like other towns, had held a St George pageant. This largely legendary soldier-saint, martyred in Palestine, had become hugely popular in western Europe at the time of the crusades. Wielder of sword and lance, he suffered a decline in popularity with advances in the use of gunpowder, but in England he was established in the popular imagination as the country's patron saint. Edward III had founded the Order of the Garter under his aegis. His day became one of the sites of conflict between Catholic and Protestant parties during the later 1500s and early 1600s, as Protestants tried to cut down on 'red-letter days' – official holy days – and Catholic influence temporarily restored them.

George is mentioned 16 times in Shakespeare, and is often called on by various warring parties in the history plays, most famously (and historically) by Henry V: 'Cry "God for Harry! England and Saint George!"' (3.1.34).

St James features indirectly and tellingly in Iago's name. St James (of Compostella) was the patron of defenders of Christianity against the Moors in Spain.

St Martin's summer (*1 Henry VI* 1.2.131) is fine weather late in the year: his feast day is 11 November.

Mary is referred to in the exclamatory word 'Marry', and in phrases such as 'By holy Mary' and 'God's holy mother' – which presumably represent everyday speech – particularly in the history plays.

'*St Nicholas* be thy speed', says Lance to Speed, challenging him to prove that he can read a letter, and calling on the patron saint of scholars (*The Two Gentlemen of Verona* 3.1.291–2).

Surprisingly, Hamlet, in a moment of emotion concerning his father's ghost, swears by *St Patrick* (1.5.135), the only direct reference to the saint in Shakespeare's work. Hamlet's murderous uncle Claudius is likened to a serpent, and perhaps Hamlet is thinking of Patrick as the saint who banished snakes from Ireland. Since Patrick is also connected with Purgatory, he may be worrying over the status of his father's spirit.

Richard III likes to swear by *St Paul* (he is the only character in Shakespeare to do so). Paul was one of the two founding saints of Christianity, and the villainous Richard's appropriation of his name is part of his offensiveness. Richard is fonder of quoting the Bible than almost any other character in the plays (he rivals only the genuinely pious Henry VI).

St Peter appears only as the keeper of the gates of heaven (*Much Ado About Nothing, Othello*).

The first and archetypal Christian martyr, *St Stephen*, who was stoned to death, is mentioned appropriately though anachronistically (the play is set in notional pre-Christian times) by the Clown to the wicked queen Tamora in the gory *Titus Andronicus* (4.4.42).

St Valentine – either one or possibly two different third-century Roman martyrs – was the patron saint of love and lovers from medieval times, either because the feast day in early spring was traditionally the day when birds paired for the season, or because it had taken over from the Roman feast of Lupercalia. Shakespeare alludes to the first of these in *A Midsummer Night's Dream*, in the words of Theseus to the waking lovers: 'Good-morrow friends. St Valentine is past; / Begin these wood-birds but to couple now?' (4.1.138–9).

AS YOU LIKE IT

c. 1599–1600

A much-loved comedy from Shakespeare's golden middle years, with the much-admired Rosalind at its centre. Banished from her uncle's court, Rosalind flees with her cousin Celia to the Forest of Arden, where her father, Duke Senior, now lives in exile. They disguise themselves for safety as brother and sister: Rosalind dresses as a boy, calling herself Ganymede. Also in the forest are the Duke's companions, including the fool, Touchstone, and Jaques, a melancholy courtier; and young Orlando, who has fled to the forest to escape his murderous brother. Head over heels in love with Rosalind, Orlando seeks advice from the spirited Ganymede, and Rosalind is hard put to it not to reveal her own love for him. In due course, true identities are revealed, arguments patched up and marriages made.

Based on a romance by Lodge, and often in lively prose, the play contrasts court and country life, favouring neither. It may have been first performed in the recently opened Globe playhouse, whose motto was reputedly *Totus mundus agit histrionem* – a sentiment made famous in the first line of Jaques's celebrated 'Seven Ages of Man' speech: 'All the world's a stage'.

First recorded performance: possibly 2 December 1603, by the King's Men, for William Herbert, 3rd Earl of Pembroke, and his guest James I at Wilton House in Wiltshire, during a plague outbreak in London.

THE COMEDY OF ERRORS

c. 1594

Egeon, a merchant from Syracuse, has come to Ephesus, despite the fact that the two cities are at enmity, in search of his son, who set out five years previously in search of his long-lost twin brother. He has been arrested and faces a death sentence, but on hearing his story the Duke allows him a day to raise a ransom. His son, Antipholus of Syracuse, has also arrived in Ephesus with his servant Dromio, and the main action of the play weaves multiple confusions between them and their brothers, Antipholus and Dromio of Ephesus, which among other elements involve Antipholus of Ephesus' wife Adriana and her sister Luciana, and a gold chain. The Syracuse twins, pursued by creditors, take refuge in a priory. Eventually all identities are revealed, including that of the Abbess, who turns out to be the wife of Egeon.

An energetically enjoyable play, at around 1,700 lines this is also the shortest Shakespeare wrote. Despite its early date, it is undeniably Shakespearean. The central plot is from Roman comedy, but Shakespeare adds to it the complicating factor of the second set of twins, the romance frame of long-lost spouses and children which anticipates his last comedies, and the setting of Ephesus, a city connected with the Christianity of St Paul, which adds a new dimension to the moral issues of the play.

First recorded performance: 28 December 1594, at Gray's Inn Hall, by a company of 'common' players, for lawyers and law students; the Inn's records note that it was performed to a packed and rowdy audience and that 'tumult' broke out.

Shakespearean names for your baby girl

Adriana	Julia
Audrey	Juliet
Beatrice	Kate
Bianca	Lavinia
Blanche	Lucetta
Celia	Mariana
Charmian	Marina
Cleopatra	Miranda
Constance	Mopsa
Cordelia	Nerissa
Cressida	Olivia
Doll	Ophelia
Dorcas	Patience
Emilia	Paulina
Gertrude	Perdita
Helena	Phoebe
Hermione	Portia
Imogen	Rosalind
Iris	Silvia
Isabel	Susanna
Isabella	Tamora
Jaquenetta	Thaisa
Jessica	Ursula
Judith	Viola

Shakespearean names for your baby boy

Adam	Horatio
Angus	Hubert
Antonio	Launcelot
Ariel	Leonardo
Arthur	Leonine
Balthazar	Lewis
Bardolph	Lucius
Bartholomew	Lysander
Bertram	Malcolm
Cassius	Nathaniel
Cato	Oberon
Clarence	Oliver
Conrade	Orlando
Corin	Orsino
Cornelius	Oswald
Edgar	Paris
Edmund	Romeo
Eros	Sebastian
Fabian	Tarquin
Ferdinand	Timon
Frederick	Titus
Gregory	Toby
Hal / Harry	Valentine
Hamlet	William

II

'Within This Wooden O'
Theatres and Players

Fig. 5. Wenceslaus Hollar's 'Long View of London' (engraved 1641)
showing the (second) Globe. The building mislabelled 'Beere bayting h.'
is in fact the Globe; the one marked 'The Globe' is the bear-baiting house.

The London theatres

Performances of plays in the later 1500s took place (like sword-fights and bull- and bear-baiting) in courtyard inns, whose design influ-enced that of the theatres that superseded them. In 1594 a ban forbade playing at city inns and allowed it only at two licensed theatres, the Rose and the Theatre. In 1600 a further ban was laid on all inn performances of any kind, and the purpose-built theatres took over. By the turn of the century, London's theatres, serving a population of around 200,000, could accommodate audiences of up to two or three thousand each.

Plays were also performed at a number of indoor venues to aristocratic audiences. They were regularly put on in the halls of the four *Inns of Court*, where young gentlemen had studied law since the thirteenth century. Audiences here would have been well educated and appreci-ative of swift wordplay. And they were performed privately to both Elizabeth I and James I. Elizabeth was particularly fond of *Greenwich Palace*, which stood downstream on the south bank of the Thames; the extensive *Whitehall Palace* in Westminster had been the main royal residence from the reign of Henry VIII. After the accession of James, a theatre enthusiast, indoor performance flourished, and a more sophisticated theatrical style involving music, spectacle and clearer division into acts and scenes became established. During James's reign Shakespeare's company performed regularly at *Hampton Court* and *Whitehall*.

Shakespeare and Elizabeth

Queen Elizabeth was supposed to have been an admirer. According to Rowe, she 'had several of his Plays Acted before her, and without doubt gave him many gracious Marks of her Favour.' She apparently particularly liked the character Falstaff in the *Henry IV* plays, and asked Shakespeare to write a play which would 'show him in Love' – the stimulus for his writing *The Merry Wives of Windsor*.

North of the Thames

The earlier – and later the more respectable – theatres were located north of the river. The Boar's Head inn in Aldgate and the Saracen's Head in Islington, north of the City, are the first London inns recorded as having been used for play performances. The Boar's Head became an official playhouse in 1598, but only survived briefly.

The Theatre

London's oldest playhouse, built in 1576 by James Burbage, and situated in Shoreditch – crucially, just outside the boundary of the City and thus beyond the reach of the disapproving City fathers. During its distinguished history it saw performances of works by Thomas Kyd, Christopher Marlowe and Shakespeare. From 1594 it was licensed solely to the Chamberlain's Men, who played there for three years until their lease expired. By then they had fallen out with the landlord, Giles Allen. In the original contract Allen owned the land while Burbage owned the theatre building. After the expiry of the lease this issue became debatable, and it was indeed a matter of contention after the Chamberlain's Men, in late 1598, dismantled the building at dead of night and removed the timbers to provide the materials for the new Globe. They took everything salvageable to Bridewell Stairs on the north bank of the Thames. The following spring, when the foundations of the new theatre were ready, the material was carried across the river to Southwark.

Blackfriars

Originally part of a Dominican monastery, this indoor theatre was leased in 1576 by Richard Farrant for performances by boy players. It was well situated near the law courts, convenient for a wealthy and fashionable clientele, and twenty years later when his lease of the Theatre was about to expire it was bought by James Burbage as a new home for the Chamberlain's Men. Objections by local residents to probable disturbance prevented its completion for this purpose. From 1600 it was rented from Richard Burbage by Henry Evans for performances by child actors and, for seven years, performances by boys' companies of biting and often highly sexual satires enjoyed a success which, along with that of Paul's Boys, threatened the takings at the Globe. After the disbanding of the boys' company in 1608 and closure in 1609 because of plague, the theatre finally returned to Burbage as the King's Men's winter home.

The Curtain

Built in Finsbury, just south of the Theatre, in 1577, this was a temporary home to the Chamberlain's Men after they left the Theatre and before their move to the Globe.

The Fortune

Opened in 1600 by Henslowe and his stepson-in-law, the actor Edward Alleyn. It was a square open-air theatre, built in St Giles without Cripplegate, by Peter Street, the master-carpenter who had just put up the Globe. Like the Globe, it was later destroyed by a fire.

South of the Thames

Bankside, a low-lying and low-life district south of the river, was notorious for its bull- and bear-baiting, its inns and its brothels. It also became home to a number of popular open-air theatres.

The Rose

A small open-air theatre near the later Globe, built in 1587 by Philip Henslowe and John Cholmley. Henslowe is best known for the 'diary' he kept from 1592 to 1609, which has survived as a uniquely important source of information on the daily business of a theatre, its schedules and finances. The Rose was for a time the home of an amalgamation of Strange's Men and the Admiral's Men (see p. 52), though in 1600 the Lord Admiral moved his company to more salubrious terrain north of the river, handing over the Rose to Pembroke's Men. By 1606 the theatre had been demolished.

The Swan

Built in 1595 in Paris Garden on Bankside, west of the Globe and Rose, by Francis Langley. After performances here of Thomas Nashe and Ben Jonson's scandalous play *The Isle of Dogs* in 1597, playing in all theatres was prohibited for a short while, and even when the general ban was lifted it continued to apply to the Swan, though it seems to have been lifted by 1602. By 1620 the theatre had dwindled into use as a venue for prize fights.

The Globe

Built in 1599 with an initial investment of £70 from each of Richard Burbage's fellow-shareholders in the Chamberlain's Men: John Hem- inges, Will Kemp, Augustine Phillips, Thomas Pope and William Shakespeare. From 1608 it was the company's summer home, and the indoor Blackfriars was used in winter. The Globe burned down on 29 June 1613 following the misfiring of a cannon into its thatch during a performance of *Henry VIII* (then called *All Is True*), but had been so successful that it was immediately rebuilt, at a cost of £1,400.

Shakespeare alludes to the Globe on several occasions. The Prologue to *Henry V* famously refers to the 'unworthy scaffold' and the 'cockpit' of 'this wooden O'; it is likely that this attention to the characteristics of the theatre was inspired by the newly opened Globe. A discussion in *Hamlet* of the boys' companies mentions that their fashionable success threatens 'Hercules and his load too' (i.e. the Globe, the world which Hercules briefly held for Atlas; 2.2, F only), and Hamlet also refers to 'this distracted globe' – the world, the theatre, and his head all at once (1.5.97).

The Hope

Another project of Henslowe's, built in 1613 on Bankside.

The Globe burns to the ground

An account of the fire by Sir Henry Wotton, in a letter to his nephew of 2 July 1613 (transcribed by the scholar E.K. Chambers). Ben Jonson was apparently also there: he mentions witnessing the event in a poem of 1623.

I will entertain you at the present with what has happened this week at the Bank's side. The King's players had a new play, called All is True, representing some principal pieces of the reign of Henry the Eighth, which was set forth with many extraordinary circumstances of pomp and majesty, even to the matting of the stage; the Knights of the Order with their Georges and garters, the Guards with their embroidered coats, and the like: sufficient in truth within a while to make greatness very familiar, if not ridiculous. Now, King Henry making a masque at the Cardinal Wolsey's house, and certain chambers being shot off at his entry, some of the paper, or other stuff, wherewith one of them was stopped, did light on the thatch, where being thought at first but idle smoke, and their eyes more attentive to the show, it kindled inwardly, and ran round like a train, consuming within less than an hour the whole house to the very grounds. This was the fatal period of that virtuous fabric, wherein yet nothing did perish but wood and straw, and a few forsaken cloaks; only one man had his breeches set on fire, that would perhaps have broiled him, if he had not by the benefit of a provident wit put it out with a bottle ale.

Hamlet all at sea

The first specifically recorded performance of *Hamlet* took place on board the East India Company ship *Red Dragon*, which was becalmed with its sister ship the *Hector* off the coast of Sierra Leone for six weeks in 1607. Captain William Keeling's diary entry for 31 September reads:

I invited Captain Hawkins to a ffishe dinner and had Hamlet acted abord me which I permit to keepe my people from idleness and unlawful games or sleepe.

The borough of Southwark

The population of London when Shakespeare's plays were being performed was probably around 200,000 and growing rapidly, especially in its suburbs, including Southwark, where prostitution and alehouses had been established for centuries. Theatres were now joining them. Jurisdiction over Southwark was divided between the City of London and the county of Surrey, and some areas had the anomalous historic status of 'liberties', allowing them to shelter debtors and fugitives from the law. It was a poor, overcrowded borough, suffering from all the concomitant problems of vagrancy, crime and high levels of infection in times of plague. As well as inns catering for the increasing numbers of visitors to the city, it was home to alehouses, theatres, brothels, prisons and bear- and bull-baiting houses. Both Philip Henslowe and Edward Alleyn were probably involved in the brothel business.

Dekker on Southwark

Thomas Dekker describes Southwark to an imaginary visitor from hell, in *Lanthorne and Candle-light* (1608).

There are more ale houses than there are taverns in all of Spain and France, the rooms as full of company as in jail. The doors of the brothels, like Hell gates stand night and day wide open, with a pair of harlots in taffeta gowns, like two painted posts, garnishing out those doors, being better to the house than a double sign.

Audiences

Audiences attending the new theatres were very mixed, and public playgoing was a hugely popular entertainment for both men and women of all classes except the Puritans and royalty. But neither Elizabeth I nor James I would have attended a public theatre.

CORIOLANUS

c. 1608

This Roman tragedy is set in the early years of the republic, almost four centuries before the death of Julius Caesar. The aristocratic Caius Martius is appointed second-in-command against the attacking Volsces. His mother Volumnia greets his appointment with fierce enthusiasm, though his wife Virgilia fears for his safety. He besieges the Volscian city of Corioles, and after victory is named Coriolanus. The Senate appoint him a consul, but he cannot humble himself to please the people: the tribunes resent his disdain and persuade the people against him. Accused of treason and banished, he approaches Aufidius, commander of the Volsces, offering to lead a Volscian army against Rome. Aufidius is warned that Coriolanus appears too powerful. Volumnia leads a delegation of women and children in an attempt to persuade Coriolanus against attack, and finally he yields. The Volscians call for his death, and Aufidius' men kill him and trample his corpse.

Audience sympathies fluctuate as the personal authority and proud talent of Coriolanus are counterpoised against vivid crowd scenes. The nature and limits of democratic power are questioned; in a famous opening scene, the body politic is compared to a physical body, in which the apparently greedy belly is vital to the health of the whole.

Coriolanus has long been a politically explosive play. Performances at the Comédie Française in Paris provoked fascist and royalist riots in 1933–4, leading to the sacking of the director and the appointment in his place of the chief of the national police. Though not popular onstage, the play was taught in schools in Nazi Germany, with Coriolanus praised as an exemplary heroic leader guiding his people towards a healthy society, and a forerunner of Adolf Hitler. It was blacklisted, along with *Julius Caesar*, by the American authorities in Germany immediately after the Second World War.

Plague

Plague was a regular event in the late sixteenth and early seventeenth centuries. It came to Stratford-upon-Avon in the winter months after William was born, when more than one in ten of the town's population died. It was then thought to spread by simple contagion, and theatres, as places of public assembly, were judged to be high risk, and were closed during outbreaks. Early in Shakespeare's career the theatres were closed in the years 1593 and 1594. Like other playwrights he had to seek other sources of income, and published two narrative poems, both dedicated to Henry Wriothesley, 3rd Earl of Southampton. The rest of his time in London was punctuated by plague closures. There was apparently no long-lasting damage to the fortunes of his company, though others suffered.

'A local habitation'

Open-air theatres

Thanks to the building of a number of replica Elizabethan theatres in modern times, we can now enter the kind of playing space that Shakespeare's audiences would have been familiar with (with added toilets and safer lighting, and without smoking and gambling during the performance), and we can try out the sense of the open, encircling space and the freedom as well as the discomfort of being a groundling.

The basic design of the open-air theatre, based on the inn courtyard which preceded it, provided a roughly circular building, with a platform stage protruding into a central yard (for standing audience members) and surrounded by galleries (for sitting or standing). Top-price spectators could buy a seat on the stage itself. The walls were created round a timber structure, with lath-and-lime plaster infilling. The encircling roof was thatched, and the stage was also roofed, probably with supporting pillars, as well as having a space below for characters such as the ghost of Hamlet's father, or for mysterious music. Behind the stage was a room or rooms from which actors made their entries, with a balcony overlooking the audience at a higher level.

There is little evidence of what the Theatre (1576) looked like; it seems to have had a turret or hut rising above it which might have covered the stage. Since the Globe (1599) was constructed from the same main timbers, it is likely that the two theatres were roughly the same size.

Fig. 6. A copy by Aernout van Buchel of the drawing of the Swan theatre made by Johannes de Witt on a visit to England, c. 1596.

The foundations of the Rose (1587) were uncovered during demolition work near the bank of the Thames in 1989. It proved to have been a small irregular 14-sided polygon, about 22 metres across, with a shallow stage. Henslowe's records show that in 1595 it acquired a 'throne in the heavens': a mechanism for lowering an actor down from the stage covering. The drawing on p. 45, made of the Swan (1595) in 1596 by a visiting Dutch scholar, Johannes de Witt, in a copy by a friend, is the only surviving representation of an open-air theatre interior of the period. It shows a theatre with more sides than the Rose – perhaps 16 to 24 – and de Witt noted that it was the largest of the London theatres. It was quite grand, with imitation painted marbling on the stage columns.

The Globe held about three thousand people, and its stage extended well into the groundlings' area. Since none of the plays written for the Globe in its early days requires a character to fly or descend, it presumably had no flight mechanism. Its exterior appearance and size, as well as the size of the Swan, are best estimated from the six-plate 'Long View of London', assembled by the Czech Wenceslaus Hollar from sketches made at the top of what is now Southwark Cathedral, and engraved, after his death, in 1641. The relevant section of the view is reproduced on page 36 – but Hollar has the labels for the Globe and the 'Beere bayting h.' (bear-baiting house) the wrong way round.

Globe prices

1*d*.	entry as a groundling
2*d*.	a seat in the galleries
3*d*.	a cushion
6*d*.	a seat in the balcony above the stage (where you became part of the spectacle)

CYMBELINE

c. 1610

The scene is ancient Britain. King Cymbeline has one surviving child, Imogen, who has married beneath her, rejecting her step-mother's loutish son Cloten. Her banished husband Posthumus, fled to Rome, undertakes a bet with Iachimo on Imogen's fidelity. Iachimo travels to Britain and creeps into Imogen's room at night, stealing a bracelet and noting a mole on her breast. Returning to Italy, he convinces Posthumus that he has been betrayed. Imogen flees to Wales where, in disguise as a boy, Fidele, she meets Guiderius and Arviragus, her brothers who were stolen at birth and until now have been unaware of their identity. Cloten pursues her, but is killed by Guiderius. Imogen takes a potion and apparently dies. Cymbeline refuses to pay tribute to Augustus Caesar and the Roman ambassador Lucius declares war. After an exceptionally complicated series of skirmishes, confusions and revelations, fractured relationships are restored and Cymbeline decides to pay the tribute.

The name Imogen makes its first appearance in the First Folio, which prints the earliest surviving text of this tragicomedy. However, it is probably a misspelling. A member of the audience at an early performance recorded the name as Innogen, a form which appears in one of Shakespeare's sources.

First recorded performance: April 1611, at the Globe, recorded in his commonplace book by Simon Forman.

Playing indoors

Blackfriars

The Blackfriars theatre, which the King's Men took over in 1608, encouraged a different kind of spectacle. Audiences tended to be predominantly better off, and their tastes and the nature of the playing space led to considerable changes in performance practice. The boys' companies which had previously played there were popular for their use of special effects, involving the flight machine and trap door, and for the high quality of their music. Their performances were divided into five acts, with musical interludes. All these features were taken up by the King's Men, and largely extended to the Globe, with results that can be seen in Shakespeare's later plays.

The room in which performances took place was rectangular, measuring about 14 by 20 metres, with the stage extending across one of the shorter ends. The walls were galleried, but the best seats here were at the front, immediately below the (fairly low) stage, and, as in the open-air theatres, on the stage itself. The indoor acoustic probably resulted in acting styles being adapted to a more intimate scale, and also meant that woodwind instruments were used, rather than the demonstrative brass which punctuated outdoor performances.

Stage directions 2: Late plays

In a number of the later plays, lengthy stage directions describe the ceremonies and dumb shows popular in the indoor theatre at Blackfriars. A long direction in *Henry VIII*, for example, gives a full listing of those taking part in the procession for the coronation of Anne Boleyn.

The Tempest provides a typical masque-like direction at 3.3.17 (the more elaborate directions in this play may have been written by the copyist Ralph Crane):

> *Solemn and strange Music: and Prosper on the top* (*invisible:*)
> *Enter several strange shapes, bringing in a Banquet; and*
> *dance about it with gentle actions of salutations, and*
> *inviting the King, etc. to eat, they depart.*

As does *The Two Noble Kinsmen* at 1.1.24:

> *Enter three Queens in black, with veils stained, with imperial*
> *crowns. The First Queen falls down at the foot of Theseus;*
> *the Second falls down at the foot of Hippolyta; the Third*
> *before Emilia.*

Censorship

Both plays and publications were subject to government censorship. Works for performance had to be approved by the Master of the Revels, an office instituted under Elizabeth I in 1581. The office-holder checked plays for material that might be considered offensive to Church or State, including indecency of situation or language, and might require alterations to be made. When the office was first established, players were obliged to perform plays in front of the Master for assessment, but as the number of plays increased this became impracticable, and he simply read the text. Publication of plays was authorised under the Bishop of London and the Arch-bishop of Canterbury until 1606, when it was taken on by George Buck, later a Master of the Revels.

The Act to Restrain Abuses of Players of 1606 forbade 'jestingly or profanely' mentioning any member of the Holy Trinity on a stage. This was applied retrospectively to plays which were revived, but not to printed publications. Some of the texts that appear in the First Folio of 1623 have undoubtedly been expurgated, though it is not clear exactly where or in what form this occurs. The Quarto version of *Othello* contains a striking number of profanities which are not in the Folio version. Were they taken out by Shakespeare in a change of heart, or removed by the censor at some point? The politically risky deposition of the king does not appear in early quartos of *Richard II* and seems a likely concession to censorship; so does the change of name of the character Sir John Oldcastle in 1 *Henry IV* to Sir John Falstaff, in response to protests by Oldcastle's descendants (Shake-speare went so far as also to change the names of Falstaff's hangers-on).

The acting companies

In the later 1500s a number of acting companies were set up under the patronage of individual aristocrats. They were largely itinerant, performing at inns, private houses, and eventually the first theatres in London. Some of them performed in Stratford-upon-Avon during Shakespeare's youth. Increasingly, at the urging of town councillors,

'Mend this'

The multi-authored play *Sir Thomas More*, which exists only in manuscript, fascinatingly reveals not only how collaborating playwrights worked together, but also the activities of the censor. The Master of the Revels, Sir Edmund Tilney, wrote marginal comments such as 'Mend this', altered mentions of Frenchmen to refer to Lombards, to avoid angering allies, and struck through most of a scene dealing with citizen insurrection in London:

> Leave out the insurrection wholly and the cause thereof, and begin with Sir Thomas More at the Mayor's sessions, with a report afterwards of his good service done being Sheriff of London upon a mutiny against the Lombards – only by a short report, and not otherwise, at your own perils.

Shakespeare was probably brought on board the project because he had experience in writing scenes depicting angry crowds which were acceptable to the censor, a skill he had demonstrated in *Julius Caesar*. His scene showing More calming the protest against foreign refugees is the finest in the play.

they were licensed. Over time they flourished, broke up and reformed; towards the end of the century a London duopoly of the Admiral's and Chamberlain's Men was established. The growing enthusiasm for playgoing led to the building of permanent playhouses in London, and this in turn led to a more established theatre by the early years of the seventeenth century.

Leicester's Men / The Queen's Men

Robert Dudley, Earl of Leicester, set up one of the first travelling companies, Leicester's Men, which in 1583 was expanded to become the Queen's Men. They flourished as a touring company round the country and in London in the 1580s, specialising in the popular new English history plays and in comedy (included among their number was the great comic actor Richard Tarlton). After the establishment in London of the Admiral's and the Chamberlain's Men in 1594 they continued to tour widely in the provinces. Shakespeare's work suggests close familiarity with the repertoire of this company, which encourages speculation that he might have been a member of it at the start of his career.

Lord Strange's / Derby's Men

The company of Ferdinando, Lord Strange, Earl of Derby, may well have included Shakespeare among its players in the early 1590s. Derby's Men performed at the Rose theatre with their leading player Edward Alleyn, who took many of the leading roles in the plays of Christopher Marlowe. They broke up after Strange's death in 1594; some of the members carried on, but Alleyn left for the Admiral's Men, and Shakespeare and others formed the Chamberlain's Men. The residue of Derby's Men dwindled, unable to compete.

Pembroke's Men

The company of Henry Herbert, 2nd Earl of Pembroke, probably included Shakespeare near the start of his career. Their repertoire included his *Titus Andronicus*, and some members of the company, including Shakespeare, later joined the Chamberlain's Men. It was their performance of Thomas Nashe and Ben Jonson's *The Isle of Dogs* that led to the temporary closure of the Swan from 1597.

The Admiral's Men

The company of the Lord Admiral, Charles Howard, Lord Effingham, was known at various times under different names. Chief rivals to the Chamberlain's Men, their playwrights included Henry Chettle, John Day (who murdered Henry Porter, another playwright), Thomas Dekker, Michael Drayton, Richard Hathway, Thomas Heywood, Anthony Munday and Robert Wilson. Edward Alleyn was a leading player with the company after leaving Lord Strange's Men.

DOUBLE FALSEHOOD

1612–13

A play called *Cardenno* or *Cardenna* was performed at court by the King's Men in 1613, at a time when Shakespeare was involved in several co-authored projects with John Fletcher. In 1653 'The History of Cardenio, by Mr Fletcher and Shakespeare' was recorded in the Stationers' Register. In 1727–8 Lewis Theobald, an editor of Shakespeare's works, published and successfully staged *Double Falsehood*, which he said he had revised and adapted from a play by Shakespeare. He claimed to have three manuscript copies of the original, but they have subsequently been lost.

The story derives from Cervantes' *Don Quixote*, a new work (1605) which quickly appeared in English translation in 1612. Cervantes' complex, multi-layered story of Cardenio is heavily simplified, and Don Quixote himself excised. The 'double falsehood' is that of Henriquez, who both pursues and rapes a maid, Violante, and pays court to Leonora, intended bride of his friend Julio (Cardenio in earlier versions of the story). Violante disguises herself as a shepherd boy and Leonora takes refuge in a nunnery. Henriquez's elder brother Roderick helps bring everything to a happy conclusion. The emphasis on reconciliation and marriage, the move to pastoral in the later scenes of the play, the foregrounding of fathers and the reunion of parents with children are themes found in many of Shakespeare's works, especially the later plays, suggesting either Shakespearean origins or the influence of Shakespeare on later adapters.

Double Falsehood, some scholars believe, is likely to represent a part of Shakespeare's oeuvre, albeit in a heavily 'restored' form adapted more than once. Richard Proudfoot, one of the General Editors of the Arden Shakespeare, suggests that it should have a place somewhere 'in the reimagined Works of William Shakespeare', even if no individual line is precisely his as it stands.

The Chamberlain's Men / King's Men

Shakespeare's company was formed in 1594 by James Burbage under the patronage of Henry Carey, then Lord Chamberlain. It was made up of a number of distinguished and successful actors from other dismantled or reorganised companies. After Henry Carey's death the patronage passed to his son George, who not long afterwards also became Lord Chamberlain. The company played at the Theatre until the expiry of their lease in 1597, and after an uncomfortable period of touring and temporary accommodation established themselves at the Globe in 1599.

On 19 May 1603, very shortly after his accession, James I became the company's patron, and they became the King's Men. From then on they played more frequently at court, and also toured more often. They were already very successful, and their position as leading company was now firmly established. In 1608 they set up a syndicate to run the indoor theatre at the Blackfriars theatre, which became their winter home from 1609. The company survived the burning down of the Globe and its rebuilding, and carried on till all theatres were closed by order of Parliament on the eve of the Civil War in 1642.

Boys' companies

Paul's Boys, the choirboys of St Paul's Cathedral, played in the cathedral grounds and did not need a licence from the Master of the Revels. They were thus able to put on more risqué plays. Boys' companies became very fashionable in the early 1600s, and formed and reformed in rapid succession. The Children of the Chapel, playing at Blackfriars from around 1600, were temporarily closed down in 1608 after incurring the displeasure of James I with their performance of George Chapman's *Conspiracy and Tragedy of Charles, Duke of Byron*.

Sharers and housekeepers

Although they enjoyed the patronage first of two Lord Chamberlains, father and son, and then of James I, the Chamberlain's/King's Men probably owed their enduring success to the fact that from the time of the establishment of the Globe they were an actors' company. Actors who were permanent members or 'sharers' of the company helped finance expenditure and in return received a share of the profits. When James Burbage's sons Richard and Cuthbert needed to finance the building of the new theatre, as well as their father's recent investment in the Blackfriars theatre, they set up a syndicate of 'housekeepers', drawn from among the sharers, each of whom contributed £70. Housekeepers were thus not only sharers in the company but also part-owners of the theatre building and business. Shakespeare was one of their number; the others were John Heminges, Will Kemp, Augustine Phillips and Thomas Pope. Will Kemp left early on – he appears to have fallen out with the company during the building of the Globe. On Pope's death in 1603 William Sly took his place, and when Phillips died in 1605 Henry Condell, already a sharer, also became a housekeeper.

A second syndicate was set up in 1608 to manage Blackfriars, now restored to the company's use; this involved the Burbages, Heminges, Shakespeare, Henry Condell, William Sly and Thomas Evans. The company was in a position to rebuild the Globe after its destruction by fire in 1613, and also survived the retirement of Shakespeare, who was replaced as chief playwright in the first instance by the prolific John Fletcher. When Richard Burbage died in 1619 only Heminges and Condell of the original group remained, and it was these two who were to publish the collected works of Shakespeare in the First Folio of 1623.

Actors

The sharers in the theatre companies, who were owners sharing in the profits, were also generally actors, though quite possibly not the company's star players. The rest of the company was made up of hired

The Names of the Principall Actors
in all thefe Playes.

WIlliam Shakefpeare.	Samuel Gilburne.
Richard Burbadge.	Robert Armin.
John Hemmings.	William Oftler.
Auguftine Phillips.	Nathan Field.
William Kempt.	John Underwood.
Thomas Poope.	Nicholas Tooley.
George Bryan.	William Ecclestone.
Henry Condell.	Jofeph Taylor.
William Slye.	Robert Benfield.
Richard Cowly.	Robert Goughe.
John Lowine.	Richard Robinfon.
Samuell Croffe.	Iohn Shancke.
Alexander Cooke.	Iohn Rice.

Fig. 7. The principal actors in the King's Men, as listed in the First Folio of 1623.

actors, and apprentices (boys who took women's and children's roles). Minor roles would be extensively doubled. Being an actor had its advantages. In the late 1590s, at a time of uncertainty with the fear of a new Spanish Armada, and an Irish rebellion, actors had the privilege of being exempt from military service.

Actors with the Chamberlain's Men/King's Men who are known to have performed in Shakespeare's plays are listed on the following pages. This may give an idea of how far Shakespeare wrote to actors' strengths (possible rather than certain roles are in a lighter type).

The male lead

Richard Burbage (*c.* 1568–1619) was the son of James Burbage, actor, theatre builder and owner. Richard was acting from the mid-1580s, and advanced to lead the Chamberlain's Men at his father's playhouse, the Theatre. He acted in plays by Ben Jonson, Thomas Kyd, John Webster and John Marston as well as Shakespeare. He was also a painter, and it has been suggested that he might have painted the Chandos portrait of Shakespeare.

Richard III

(the role in which Burbage apparently made his name)

Brutus, *Julius Caesar*
Hamlet
Othello
King Lear

Shakespeare and Burbage

Recorded in the journal of a law student, John Manningham, in 1602:

Upon a time when Burbage played Richard III, there was a citizen grown so far in liking with him, that before she went from the play she appointed him to come that night unto her by the name of Richard III. Shakespeare, overhearing their conclusion, went before, was entertained, and at his game ere Burbage came. Then message being brought that Richard III was at the door, Shakespeare caused return to be made that William the Conqueror was before Richard III.

John Lowin (1576–1653) became a member of the King's Men in 1603. A big man, he seems to have specialised in such physically substantial roles as Henry VIII, Volpone, Sir Epicure Mammon and Falstaff.

Henry VIII
Falstaff

John Heminges (1566–1630) was a successful manager as well as actor; he was one of the first group of Globe 'housekeepers', and by the end of his career was effectively in charge of the King's Men. He seems to have played older characters.

Julius Caesar
Polonius, *Hamlet*
Falstaff

Augustine Phillips (d. 1605)

Bolingbroke, *Richard II*
King Henry, *1, 2 Henry IV*

Joseph Taylor joined the King's Men in 1619 and succeeded Richard Burbage as principal male lead, taking roles including Hamlet, Iago and possibly Palamon or Arcite in *The Two Noble Kinsmen*.

Shakespeare was also undoubtedly influenced by the celebrated *Edward Alleyn* (1566–1626), actor with Worcester's Men, Strange's Men and the Admiral's (subsequently Prince Henry's) Men. Alleyn was particularly admired for his portrayals of the forceful and charismatic protagonists of Marlowe's great plays – *Tamburlaine, The Jew of Malta* and *Doctor Faustus* – and for his demonstrative acting style and ringing delivery. He was probably also physically big. These were roles and an acting style which Shakespeare had to come to terms with – he probably both admired and mocked them (as Hamlet does the First Player). Alleyn was son-in-law to Philip Henslowe, and in due course Henslowe's Diary was left to the College of God's Gift which Alleyn founded at Dulwich in 1619.

HAMLET

c. 1600

Hamlet, a revenge play in the fashionable style of the 1590s, following Kyd's *Spanish Tragedy*, was Shakespeare's third tragedy, preceded only by *Titus Andronicus* and *Romeo and Juliet*. Nonetheless it is perhaps the most archetypal of all tragedies, and certainly the most influential of Shakespeare's works. Hamlet, Prince of Denmark, learns from his father's ghost that his uncle Claudius murdered his father before marrying Hamlet's mother, Gertrude. Hamlet feels he has just cause to avenge the murder, but cannot make up his mind to do so, and delays till the end of the play. The gap between thought and action displays an awareness of individual consciousness that has engaged audiences and readers over four centuries.

Distracted by his own thoughts, Hamlet seems to those around him to be going mad. He spurns Ophelia, arranges the performance of a play mirroring Claudius' and Gertrude's crimes, argues with his mother and, half-unwittingly, kills Ophelia's father, Polonius. Ophelia goes mad and drowns herself. Hamlet contemplates the skull of Yorick in the graveyard. The drama ends in a bloodbath of poisoning and swordplay which leaves all the main characters dead and the sorrowing Fortinbras successor, with Hamlet's 'dying voice', to the throne of Denmark.

The play has inspired continuing fascination with and debate about the character of Hamlet, his madness and delay, and all around the world has been seen as a powerful representation of the dilemmas faced by those living under oppressive rule.

For the first recorded performance, see p. 41.

The comic lead

Shakespeare's earlier lead comic roles were taken by **William Kemp** (d. 1603). Kemp was clown with the Lord Chamberlain's Men from 1594 to 1599, but seems to have parted company with them during the construction of the Globe in Southwark. He was a formidably popular comedian, and an enthusiastic morris dancer who after leaving the Globe danced his way from London to Norwich, a feat recorded in 1600 in *Kemp's Nine Days' Wonder*. In several instances in the earlier plays his entries or speeches are noted under his own name rather than that of the character he played, presumably because he was so well known. He seems not to have flourished after leaving the Globe, and died in poverty only a few years later.

Peter, *Romeo and Juliet*
Dogberry, *Much Ado About Nothing*
Lance, *The Two Gentlemen of Verona*
Clown, *Titus Andronicus*
Costard, *Love's Labour's Lost*
Bottom, *A Midsummer Night's Dream*
Lancelot, *The Merchant of Venice*
Falstaff, *1, 2 Henry IV* and *The Merry Wives of Windsor*

With the departure of Kemp, the role of the clown changed. His successor (formerly of Chandos's Men) was **Robert Armin** (*c.* 1568–1615) – a more verbal, intellectual and biting wit, as the roles Shakespeare wrote for him indicate, and an accomplished singer, as well as a playwright himself. After he joined the company, Shakespeare's fools and melancholy riddlers seemed to find their full potential.

Touchstone, *As You Like It*
Feste, *Twelfth Night*
Thersites, *Troilus and Cressida*
Lavatch, *All's Well That Ends Well*
Gravedigger, *Hamlet*
The Fool, *King Lear*

Richard Cowley (c. 1568–1619)

Verges, *Much Ado About Nothing*

John Sincler or Sinklo (a hired actor; also Pembroke's Men)

A player, *The Taming of the Shrew*
Nym, *2 Henry IV*, *Henry V*, *The Merry Wives of Windsor*
Sinklo, a gamekeeper, *3 Henry VI*
Apothecary, *Romeo and Juliet*
Robin Starveling, *A Midsummer Night's Dream*
Slender, *The Merry Wives of Windsor*
Robert Faulconbridge, *King John*
A beadle, *2 Henry IV*
Sir Andrew Aguecheek, *Twelfth Night*

Not to mention the dog

Lance's dog in *The Two Gentlemen of Verona* was probably an early theatrical canine scene-stealer. When asked if a match will be made between Proteus and Julia, Lance replies: 'Ask my dog: if he say "ay", it will; if he say "no", it will; if he shake his tail, and say nothing, it will' (2.5.31–2).

Minor roles

The presumed practice of using the actor's name for the entry direction or speech prefix in very minor roles (rather than Player, etc.), led to the otherwise apparently random naming of bit-part characters such as Sinklo or Gabriel and no doubt others. *John Sincler*, probably a hired actor rather than a 'sharer' in the King's Men, is suggested in this way for a number of small parts. His apparent skinniness has suggested a number of other roles he might have taken. *Gabriel Spencer* (1576–98), of Pembroke's Men and the Admiral's Men, apparently played a messenger (Gabriel) in *3 Henry VI*. He eventually enjoyed the greater but unfortunate distinction of being killed by Ben Jonson in a duel – he had himself stabbed a man to death two years earlier.

Prompt-book copy may be the source of the text where such names appear. Another example is someone called Tawyer, who entered at the head of the actors coming on to perform 'Pyramus and Thisbe' in *A Midsummer Night's Dream*: '*Tawyer with a trumpet before them*' (5.1.125). A *William Tawyer* appears in a 1624 list of the King's Men's musicians.

John Heminges (1566–1630) and *Henry Condell* (1576–1627) are now chiefly remembered as the pair jointly responsible for the publication of the First Folio. Condell was a sharer in the Lord Chamberlain's Men, and an actor who appeared with Richard Burbage in several of Ben Jonson's plays. Heminges was business manager for the King's Men, and also an actor.

Stage directions 3: Enter the ghost in his nightgown

Descriptions of dress may be crucial for the action – as when a character enters disguised – or may record historical performance practice:

Enter Duke Senior and Lord, like Out-laws.   *As You Like It* 2.7

Enter sir Iohn with a buck's head upon him.
                            The Merry Wives of Windsor 5.5

Enter Rumour painted full of tongues.   *2 Henry IV* 1.1
        (*an appearance by a popular traditional medieval figure*)

Enter Coriolanus in a gown of Humility . . .   *Coriolanus* 2.3.39

Enter the Duchess in a white sheet, and a Taper burning in her hand . . .   *2 Henry VI* 2.4.16

Enter the Queen with her hair about her ears . . .
                                    Richard III 2.2.33

Enter Richard and Buckingham, in rotten Armour, marvellous ill-favoured.   *Richard III* 3.5

Enter Ariel invisible.   *The Tempest* 3.2.39

Cross-dressing

Shakespeare's comic heroines are almost synonymous in the popular view with cross-dressing. Several of his best-loved roles originally involved a boy actor playing a woman who disguises herself as a young man. Shakespeare's first try at this was with the role of Julia (*The Two Gentlemen of Verona*) in the early 1590s, but the most famous examples date from around the turn of the century. Perhaps it was a response to theatrical fashion and public demand. It is hard to believe that it was simply a matter of convenience, devised to avoid the difficulty of presenting not very feminine boys as women, since boys appear to have performed tragic roles such as Ophelia with success. More likely is that the additional sexual ambiguity of the relationship between the disguised heroine and 'her' young aristocratic lover, as well as her role in the mainly male world surrounding her, was enjoyably, if covertly, homoerotic. Shakespeare followed his source, Thomas Lodge, in taking the name Ganymede (in classical mythology Jove's cupbearer) for his almost androgynous Rosalind in disguise; it is a name that at the time would have been shadowed by the word 'catamite', which derived from it.

At the same time, the heroines who resulted from the boy-actor tradition are as memorable for their spirit, intelligence and wit as are, in their own way, the heroines of Jane Austen, and they continue to offer modern actresses some of their finest roles. 'Ganymede' also, in Renaissance thinking, emblematised 'intelligence and rational thought'.

Boy actors

Women were not allowed to appear on the public stage in early modern England, and female roles in the theatre were taken by apprentice actors. Puberty was often not reached until the mid to late teens, and boy actors were aged between fourteen and eighteen years, when they would have been more intellectually mature than the modern-day equivalent of twelve or thirteen. There would have been relatively few boys in a company – normally no more than five – and the peak of an individual's career would have been brief. There was perhaps only one at any one time capable of sustaining a major role such as Cleopatra or Rosalind. (And perhaps there was no one very good around when Shakespeare wrote only 11 lines for female characters in *Timon of*

Athens.) The boy who played both Cleopatra and Lady Macbeth must have been a considerable actor; he is likely to have been a different one from the actor of a different temperament for whom Shakespeare probably wrote the roles of Ophelia, Desdemona and Viola.

Unfortunately, little is known about individual boy actors. Some of their names are known, but no roles can be specifically attributed.

Did actors have scripts?

Two-thirds of the male population in England in 1600, and somewhere between 80 and 90 per cent of women, were functionally illiterate, though literacy in London was higher (around 60 per cent of men). Both John and Mary Shakespeare signed legal documents with a mark, though this was quite common practice in trade, and is not necessarily an indication of illiteracy. Susanna, Shakespeare's daughter, could certainly write. Apart from bit-players, actors must have been able to read, and anyone taking on a more substantial role would have needed to be very competent with a script. Boys apprenticed as actors may well have been better educated than some of the adult actors (certainly Paul's Boys would have been well educated), and would have benefited also from their training in the theatres. Evidently some of them were very effective at portraying clever women.

The mechanicals in *A Midsummer Night's Dream* appear to be more or less literate. Peter Quince, the manager, is thoroughly at home with the written word and able to draw up a list of properties required; he is presumably the author of all or part of their play. Snug the joiner, on the other hand, asks anxiously for his part in good time, because he is 'slow of study'; he is reassured that he can do it without, since it is 'nothing but roaring' (1.2.64–6). Individual parts were written on rolls of paper, and consisted of the single part with cues – Bottom informs Theseus that '"Deceiving me" is Thisbe's cue' (5.1.182–3).

JULIUS CAESAR

1599

Julius Caesar has just defeated Pompey, and some in the Roman republic fear he may declare himself king; a group of conspirators, including Cassius and Brutus, plot his assassination. A soothsayer warns him to beware the Ides of March, and his wife Calpurnia begs him not to go to the Capitol. He is persuaded to ignore her advice, and is stabbed by the conspirators, including, finally – '*Et tu, Brute?*' – Brutus. Mark Antony addresses the plebeians at Caesar's funeral, arousing their anger with ironic praise for the conspirators. Caesar's ghost appears to Brutus before he and Cassius meet Antony and Caesar's nephew Octavius in battle. The conspirators are defeated and Brutus falls on his sword.

The play deliberately leaves open to question whether Brutus is to be seen as a freedom-fighting republican or a cold-blooded zealot. Dealing (not unlike the contemporaneous *Hamlet* – though the element from the sources omitted by Shakespeare is that Brutus was probably Caesar's illegitimate son) with the issue of whether it is right to kill a tyrant, the play is perennially topical, and has often been performed in times and places when direct political criticism is risky.

First recorded performance: 21 September 1599, in a 'straw-thatched house', recorded by a Swiss visitor to London, Thomas Platter. For a notorious Brutus, see p. 189.

Shakespearean heroines

Comic heroines

Early 1590s

Katherina
(*The Taming of the Shrew*)

Julia, disguised as 'Sebastian'
(*The Two Gentlemen of Verona*)

Adriana (*The Comedy of Errors*)

Mid- to late-1590s

Rosaline (*Love's Labour's Lost*)

Helena and Hermia
(*A Midsummer Night's Dream*)

Portia, disguised as
a young lawyer, 'Balthazar'
(*The Merchant of Venice*)

Mistress Ford, Mistress Page
and Mistress Quickly
(*The Merry Wives of Windsor*)

Beatrice
(*Much Ado About Nothing*)

Late 1599, early 1600s

Rosalind, disguised as
'Ganymede' (*As You Like It*)

Viola, disguised as 'Cesario'
(*Twelfth Night*)

Olivia (*Twelfth Night*)

Helena
(*All's Well That Ends Well*)

Isabella (*Measure for Measure*)

1607–14

Marina (long-lost) (*Pericles*)

Perdita (long-lost)
(*The Winter's Tale*)

Hermione (disguised as a statue)
(*The Winter's Tale*)

Imogen, disguised as 'Fidele'
(*Cymbeline*)

Miranda (exiled) (*The Tempest*)

Tragic heroines

Early 1590s

Lavinia (*Titus Andronicus*)

Tamora (*Titus Andronicus*)

Mid- to late-1590s

Juliet (*Romeo and Juliet*)

Late 1599, early 1600s

Ophelia (*Hamlet*)

Gertrude (*Hamlet*)

Cressida (*Troilus and Cressida*)

Desdemona (*Othello*)

Cordelia (*King Lear*)

Goneril and Regan (*King Lear*)

Lady Macbeth (*Macbeth*)

Cleopatra
(*Antony and Cleopatra*)

Volumnia (*Coriolanus*)

1608–14

Emilia (*The Two Noble Kinsmen*)

Historical heroines

Early 1590s
Joan Puzel (*1 Henry VI*)
Queen Margaret (*1, 2, 3 Henry VI, Richard III*)
Queen Elizabeth (*3 Henry VI, Richard III*)
Lady Anne (*Richard III*)

Mid- to late-1590s
Queen Isabel (*Richard II*)
Constance (*King John*)

Late 1599, early 1600s
Princess Katherine (*Henry V*)

1608–14
Queen Katherine *(Henry VIII)*
Anne Boleyn (*Henry VIII*)

Who is Rosaline?

Two of Shakespeare's brightest heroines, and Romeo's first love, share versions of the same name:

- Rosaline, a lady attendant on the Princess of France, is the quick-witted heroine of *Love's Labour's Lost*.
- Rosalind, banished by her usurping uncle Duke Frederick, flees with her cousin Celia to the Forest of Arden, disguised as a boy. She is in love with Orlando (*As You Like It*). The Folio text sometimes spells her 'Rosaline'.
- Rosaline is the unattainable beloved of Romeo before he sets eyes on Juliet; she is not mentioned in stage directions, though some productions have included her in the gathering at the Capulets' ball (*Romeo and Juliet*).

Shakespeare's ghosts

'Angels and ministers of grace defend us!'

Shakespeare's onstage ghosts are few, but they include three of the most famous ghosts in all drama. It is not clear – except in theatrical terms – whether they are 'actually' present or whether they exist only in the minds of the beholders, but their 'appearance' bears witness to crimes and guilt and spurs the living to revenge.

Ghosts in Elizabethan and Jacobean drama owed more to the popular imagination and to models of classical Roman drama than to the Protestant view, which was problematic: spirits would not return, it was believed, and anything that appeared to be one was a trick of the devil. Ghosts and ghostly events (such as squeaking and gibbering in the Roman streets) are serious portents and indications of great wrongs that must be righted.

'Be thou a spirit of health, or goblin damned'

Julius Caesar
Hamlet's Father
Banquo

'Despair and die'

On the eve of Richard III's defeat and death at the battle of Bosworth, a flock of ghosts – all of them his victims – appears in succession in his sleep. They serve as witnesses and reminders of Richard's crimes and emphasise that his defeat is a just revenge on tyranny.

Prince Edward
King Henry VI
The Duke of Clarence
Lady Anne
Lord Rivers and Lord Grey, Sir Thomas Vaughan
Two young Princes, sons of King Edward IV
The Duke of Buckingham

❧ *Vows* ❧

'Tis not the many oaths that makes the truth,
But the plain single vow that is vowed true.

All's Well That Ends Well 4.2.21–2

I do love you more than word can wield the matter,
Dearer than eyesight, space and liberty.

King Lear 1.1.55–6

I swear to thee by Cupid's strongest bow,
By his best arrow with the golden head,
By the simplicity of Venus' doves,
By that which knitteth souls and prospers loves.

A Midsummer Night's Dream 1.1.169–72

I will live in thy heart, die in thy lap, and be buried in thy eyes –
and moreover, I will go with thee to thy uncle's.

Much Ado About Nothing 5.2.93–5

My bounty is as boundless as the sea,
My love as deep: the more I give to thee
The more I have, for both are infinite.

Romeo and Juliet 2.2.133–5

Such is my love, to thee I so belong,
That for thy right myself will bear all wrong.

Sonnet 88.13–14

Kiss me, Kate, we will be married o'Sunday.

The Taming of the Shrew 2.1.328

Hear my soul speak:
The very instant that I saw you did
My heart fly to your service.

The Tempest 3.1.63–5

I would not wish
Any companion in the world but you.

The Tempest 3.1.54–5

Stage directions 4:
Enter Imogen in her bed, and a Lady

Props may be essential for the furtherance of the plot; and directions may set the scene, on an otherwise more or less unfurnished stage:

Macbeth's Wife alone with a letter.   *Macbeth* 1.5
(*The letter, from Macbeth, reports the witches' prophecies of his future greatness*)

Drum and colours. Enter Malcolm, Siward, Macduff, and their Army, with Boughs.   *Macbeth* 5.6
(*Birnam Wood comes to Dunsinane*)

Enter a Company of Mutinous Citizens, with Staves, Clubs and other weapons.   *Coriolanus* 1.1
(*This opening direction sets the tone for the play*)

Enter two Officers, to lay Cushions, as it were, in the Capitol.
Coriolanus 2.2

They march about the Stage, and Servingmen come forth with their napkins.   *Romeo and Juliet* 1.5

KING EDWARD III

c. 1592–4

The authorship of *Edward III* is not known, but the only dramatist
whose involvement is based on substantial evidence is Shakespeare.
The play falls into two halves. The first presents Edward at war in
Scotland, and wooing the Countess of Salisbury (doubly adul-
terously, since both parties are married); in the second England is
fighting the French, and the king is happily reunited with his son,
the Black Prince, who had been thought killed in battle.
Shakespeare's likely involvement is clearest in the scenes relating to
the Countess of Salisbury, which are also the most effective in the
play. Beyond this the nature and extent of his contribution are likely
to remain in dispute, along with the identity of his co-author/s.

KING HENRY IV, PART I

1596–7

This hugely popular play, printed in at least seven quartos before the First Folio, was the first of Shakespeare's histories plotted in parallel worlds of high politics and low comedy. Henry IV has two rebellions on his hands: an insurgent group including Henry Hotspur, Owen Glendower and Mortimer; and his son, Prince Hal, who to his father's despair haunts the Boar's Head Tavern in Eastcheap and consorts with lowlife, in particular the fat knight Sir John Falstaff (originally Oldcastle – the name had to be changed to avoid trouble with the descendants of the real Sir John Oldcastle). Hal is torn between two father figures. His behaviour is disreputable, involving drinking, duplicity and unsavoury escapades, but it becomes clear that he will finally shoulder his responsibilities. His future rejection of Falstaff is foreshadowed in a scene where he and Falstaff act out an imaginary father–son encounter between Hal and Henry, each playing each role in turn. Henry compares Hal unfavourably with the valorous and energetic Hotspur, but in the concluding battle of Shrewsbury Hal shows himself Hotspur's match in courage and a man of judgement and generosity.

The play is Falstaff's as much as Hal's, and he is the main reason to perform it. Fat, venal and bursting with life in the comic tavern scenes, he is an effective contrast to officially prescribed heroism in his frankly self-interested cowardice and duplicity on the battle-field.

First recorded performance: 1600, in the presence of the Flemish ambassador.

KING HENRY IV, PART 2
1597–8

The second *Henry IV* play, written shortly after the first, reflects its predecessor in darker tones. The rebels have lost the battle of Shrewsbury and Hotspur has been killed, but they are not yet defeated, and Henry's armies are fighting on various fronts. Prince Hal is secretly troubled by his father's illness, and Henry lies on his sickbed worrying about his son and his country. Once again, though, it is Falstaff's play. He also is sick, and being short of money, attempts to raise cash by taking bribes for exemption from military service. Hal, in disguise, hears Falstaff disparage him. Falstaff and his old cronies Justice Shallow and Justice Silence remember better days. At his sleeping father's bedside Hal believes that Henry has died, and puts on the crown; Henry wakes and censures him, but eventually the two are reconciled. Henry advises his son to engage in foreign wars to prevent rebellion at home.

Henry dies. Falstaff attends Henry V's coronation procession, expecting a golden future, but in a scene which arouses feelings of pathos, regret and inevitability, the new king repudiates him and renounces his past, saying 'I know thee not, old man'.

First recorded performance: during the winter season of 1612–13, with *1 Henry IV*, as part of the wedding celebrations for Princess Elizabeth and the Elector Palatine.

Top ten heroines

ROSALIND
most likely to be fallen in love with

BEATRICE
wittiest

VIOLA
most melancholy

JULIET
most romantic

PORTIA
posh and brainy

OPHELIA
most iconic

KATHERINA
sparkiest

ISABELLA
integrity, strength of mind

PERDITA
loveliest

CLEOPATRA
most seductive

Top ten heroes

HAMLET
moody, sexy, clever, flawed

ROMEO
most romantic

HENRY V
most heroic

PETRUCCIO
most outrageous

BENEDICK
wittiest

MERCUTIO
most poetic

PERICLES
most moving survivor

EDGAR
most decent

PROSPERO
wisest

FALSTAFF
most imperfect

III

'Devise, Wit; Write, Pen'

Controversies: Authorship, Sonnets and Texts

The authorship controversy

Surprisingly, since the concept is now very familiar, the questioning of authorship by the man from Stratford did not publicly arise until the mid-nineteenth century, when in 1852 an anonymous writer in *Chambers' Edinburgh Journal* suggested that Shakespeare 'kept a poet'. The author was not alone in feeling that the somewhat grouchy and litigious provincial figure suggested by the sparse documentary evidence of Shakespeare's life could not have been the divine creator of England's greatest plays, whose author must have been a well-educated aristocrat or gentleman rather than a lowly actor. Recent linguistic evidence in Shakespeare's favour is overwhelming and decisive; and Jonson's prefatory verses in the First Folio refer to the 'Sweet Swan of Avon'. However, the subject will probably never now be fully quashed.

The Baconian Theory and Delia Bacon

Francis Bacon, 1st Baron Verulam and Viscount St Albans (1561–1627) was a lawyer, politician and the greatest philosopher of his day. He was the author of the first – and very fine – published essays in the English language, and also of a few minor dramatic works. His authorship of the Shakespeare oeuvre is first known to have been contemplated by a clergyman, the Rev. James Wilmot, in 1785. Wilmot did not publish his views, however, and the Bacon theory was first properly proposed (with Walter Ralegh and Edmund Spenser as joint authors) in 1856, and a year later in a volume entitled *The Philosophy of the Plays of Shakspere Unfolded*, by Delia Bacon, a teacher and writer from Ohio who in due course died insane. It was more fully expounded in 1857 by William Henry Smith in his book *Bacon and Shakespeare*. Smith found textual similarities between Bacon's writings and the 'Shakespeare' plays, and argued that Bacon would have concealed his authorship because acknowledging it would have been unacceptable given his social position.

Hidden links to Bacon in the Shakespeare works have been discovered by many allegory-hunters since. According to Dr Orville Ward Owen, the inventor of a decoding machine for furthering this process and author of the five-volume *Sir Francis Bacon's Cipher Story* (1893–5), close study reveals that Bacon encoded his true parentage in the plays – he was the son of Elizabeth I and the Earl of Leicester.

The Oxfordian Theory and Thomas Looney

The claim for *Edward de Vere, 17th Earl of Oxford* (1550–1604) first appeared in 1827 in a novel by Robert Plumer Ward, *De Vere, or the Man of Independence*. The suggestion was not picked up. In 1920 an English schoolmaster, Thomas Looney, who – unfamiliar with conventional poetic forms – had been struck by the similarities between brief verses by Oxford and the stanzaic form of *Venus and Adonis*, published '*Shakespeare' Identified*. Looney, again, was troubled at the idea that an actor from a humble background and with a plebeian taste in lawsuits might be capable of greatness.

It was clear even early on that the Earl of Oxford – a violent and dissolute man who murdered a servant at the age of seventeen, and an unattractive candidate – was not a likely contender, despite an interest in the theatre which led him to be patron of a players' company, Oxford's Men, from the 1580s. In practical terms alone, his death in 1604 leaves his advocates with some awkward matters to confront, though detailed and valiant explanations have been offered.

Oxford was a writer, but his verses tend to suggest that he was not the author of the Shakespeare plays. He was fond of the heptameter, a seven-footed line also known as the 'fourteener', which Shakespeare most often used for comic effect. Its straightforward, non-ironical use by Oxford provides one of the arguments against his claim to the authorship of Shakespeare's plays. As with Bacon, his backers have come up with distinguished secret connections for their man. Charles and Dorothy Ogburn claimed in 1952 that he had secretly married Elizabeth I, and that the Earl of Southampton – identified as the fair youth of the sonnets – was their son.

Oxford is still a popular candidate and his case is keenly fought on both sides.

The Marlovian Theory

Shakespeare's close contemporary, the playwright *Christopher Marlowe* (1564–93), is a perfect subject for conspiracy theorists. On the face of it he is disqualified by his (well-documented) early death in a Deptford tavern, right at the beginning of the period to which the 'Shakespeare' plays can be dated. However, the circumstances of his death have only proved an inspiration to speculation, and adherents propose that it was faked. William Gleason Zeigler, a San Francisco lawyer, suggested in his novel of 1895, *It Was Marlowe: A Story of the Secret of Three Centuries*, that Marlowe had escaped death, lived a further five years in hiding, and written most of the Shakespeare oeuvre during that rather brief time. The theory was given a new lease of life in 1955 by another American, Calvin Hoffman, who in *The Murder of the Man Who Was Shakespeare* outlined a complicated theory involving Sir Francis Walsingham, head of the secret service, as Marlowe's secret homosexual lover, faking Marlowe's death and passing off his plays as the work of the jobbing actor William Shakespeare.

The many other candidates include

Elizabeth I, James I,
William Stanley, 6th Earl of Derby, John Florio,
Roger Manners, 5th Earl of Rutland,
Mary Herbert, Countess of Pembroke

Famous doubters of Shakespeare of Stratford's authorship include

Lord Palmerston, Ralph Waldo Emerson, Herman Melville,
the distinguished scholar Dr W.H. Furness, Mark Twain,
Prince Otto von Bismarck, Sigmund Freud

Those who argue that a provincial actor with a middle-class grammar-school education could not have acquired the range of learning and skills necessary to compose the Shakespeare oeuvre need look no further, as Jonathan Bate has suggested, than the far more academic plays of Ben Jonson, who was the stepson of a bricklayer, and had also had no more than a good 'secondary' level education.

The Sonnets and the 'onlie begetter'

Shakespeare's sonnets have attracted voluminous attention; both because of the depth and complexity of the writing, and on account of the uncertain circumstances of their creation and the apparently personal nature of their content. They appear to be addressed to two people, a young man and a 'dark' woman. The identity of these two has been endlessly debated, without conclusion.

Shakespeare's earliest London successes were also enduring ones – two long poems, *Venus and Adonis* and *The Rape of Lucrece*, written for his patron, the young Henry Wriothesley, 3rd Earl of Southampton, in the 1590s while the theatres were closed, and published to wide acclaim and financial success. These two poems and the sonnets constitute most of his non-dramatic work. The sonnets were written over a number of years, probably for a patron, as almost all poetry was, rather than simply for general publication. At the same time, at least some of them were circulated in the 1590s among the author's 'private friends'. Two were published in a pirated collection without Shakespeare's consent, and 154 eventually appeared in a quarto edition in 1609. This volume was not reprinted, and seems, strangely, to have caused little comment. Comparisons between versions of the same sonnet printed some years apart suggest that the author may have regarded them as work in progress – or they may simply be poor texts.

The poems printed in the First Quarto appear to be intentionally ordered. Sonnets 1–126 seem to be addressed to a young man, and the next twenty-six to a woman of dark complexion. The last two sonnets, on the subject of Venus and Adonis, are unconnected with the rest.

The first seventeen sonnets urge the young man to procreate – not to leave the world without a copy of his fair self – and Sonnets 18–126 (the remainder of the group) deal with the young man, with a woman who may be mistress to both the addressee and the poet, with time and decay, with the addressee's coldness and faults of character, and with the poet's rivalry with other writers. The last two dozen excuse the poet's silence and disclaim his inconstancy.

Sonnets 127–52 are addressed to the poet's mistress, and bitterly discuss her unfaithfulness and their flawed relationship.

The addressees are popularly known, though not described in the sonnets themselves, as the 'fair youth' and the 'dark lady'. Unlike his contemporaries – Philip Sidney with his Astrophil and Stella, or Samuel Daniel with his Delia, for example – Shakespeare did not decorate his personae with classical or mythical names. That was a technique that made clearer the paradoxical distinction/connection between the character in the poem and the addressee. Shakespeare's unnamed players are somehow all the more intriguing. And whether or not this was any kind of a real-life love triangle we will probably never know.

In the tangle of identity, we need to remember that the patron, the addressee and the printer's dedicatee 'Mr. W.H.', who is described in the opening inscription to the Quarto as the 'onlie begetter', may refer to one of at least three different people.

Misprints 1: Mr. W.H.

Much ink has been spilled speculating on the identity of Mr. W.H., the 'onlie begetter' of the sonnets mentioned in the inscription printed at the head of the 1609 edition. The word 'begetter' is ambiguous – it more often signified 'author' than 'patron' or 'inspirer', but could also have indicated the person who handed over the manuscript. It has been suggested that 'W.H.' was a misprint originating in George Eld's printing shop. According to this theory, a compositor would have misread a contemporary handwritten capital S as an H (the two occur in similar forms), and the onlie begetter should be identified as Mr. W.S., the author.

Who's who in the Sonnets?

I: THE FAIR YOUTH – THE SHORTLIST

There are only two serious candidates for the role. Both were noted patrons to poets, both were of the social standing suggested by the texts of the sonnets, and both had family eager for them to marry, while they themselves were exceptionally reluctant. Because one was born seven years earlier than the other, preference partly depends on the favoured date of composition.

Henry Wriothesley, 3rd Earl of Southampton

Southampton (1573–1624), a distant connection of Shakespeare's mother, was undoubtedly the patron for his long narrative poems, and later anecdote credits him with supporting Shakespeare to the tune of the enormous sum of £1,000. In the early 1590s, when the first sonnets may well have been written, he would have been nineteen or twenty. Linguistic evidence and possible biographical evidence from within the sonnets is compatible with his candidacy. (Wriothesley is probably pronounced Rose-ly or Rye-ose-ly.)

William Herbert, 3rd Earl of Pembroke

Pembroke's case was put forward at the end of the nineteenth century by Sir Sidney Lee in the *Dictionary of National Biography*, though by the time he came to write his entry on Shakespeare under the letter S he

Fig. 8 (above). Henry Wriothesley, 3rd Earl of Southampton, by an unknown artist, c. 1600.
Fig. 9 (opposite page). William Herbert, 3rd Earl of Pembroke, by Isaac Oliver.

had changed his mind in favour of Southampton. Pembroke (1580–1630), a nephew of Sir Philip Sidney, was one of the dedicatees of the First Folio, and his initials are clearly W.H. He was reluctant only to marry, not to make love to women, since he was indisputably lover to several. A description of James I's coronation ceremony sent by the Venetian Secretary to the Doge in Venice includes a brief anecdote which suggests that Pembroke was exceptionally free and bold with both sexes: 'The Earl of Pembroke, a handsome youth, who is always with the King, and always joking with him, actually kissed his Majesty's face, whereupon the King laughed and gave him a little cuff.' Against his claim stands the fact that he was a very young teenager in the early 1590s, the most probable dating of the first sonnets, and that no link has been established between Shakespeare himself (as distinct from his company) and Pembroke.

Outsiders

ROBERT DEVEREUX, 2ND EARL OF ESSEX
a favourite candidate of Baconians

HAMNET SHAKESPEARE
the poet's son, who died in 1596 at the age of eleven

EDMUND SHAKESPEARE
the poet's younger brother, also an actor

FATHER ROBERT SOUTHWELL
a Catholic martyr

WILL KEMP
Shakespeare's company's clown in the 1590s –
not on the face of it a 'fair youth'

WILLIE HUGHES
In *Portrait of Mr. W.H.* (1899) Oscar Wilde cast an imaginary
boy actor as the object of Shakespeare's admiration.

Mary Fitton

Mary Fitton, a maid of honour to Queen Elizabeth, was for long thought a likely candidate as she was the mistress of the Earl of Pembroke, and disgraced mother of his illegitimate son. She appears, however, to have been fair-haired and grey-eyed.

Emilia Lanyer

Emilia Lanyer was championed by the historian A.L. Rowse in 1973, though his evidence has since been proved shaky. She was the mistress of Henry Carey, Lord Hunsdon, the Lord Chamberlain and patron of Shakespeare's company.

Anne Hathaway

Shakespeare's wife.

Jane Davenant

Mother of William Davenant, the poet and dramatist who was rumoured to be Shakespeare's illegitimate child.

Mrs Florio (née Daniel)

The wife of John Florio, a writer, grammarian and, as translator of the works of Montaigne, a lasting influence on Shakespeare's work. Florio was language tutor to Southampton and a member of his household. Mrs Florio was a sister of the poet Samuel Daniel; her case was made by Jonathan Bate in 1997.

Jacqueline Field

Wife of Richard Field, a printer originally from Stratford-upon-Avon who printed some of Shakespeare's work.

Penelope Rich

Muse of the poet Sir Philip Sidney.

Lucy Negro or Morgan

A (black?) prostitute also known as the 'Abbess of Clerkenwell'.

Queen Elizabeth

An early candidate, proposed by George Chalmers in 1797.

3: THE RIVAL POET

The rival poet is seen in the sonnets as a contender for the patronage and possibly the affections of the young man; Shakespeare feels 'inferior far' to this poet with a 'worthier pen'. Some have taken him to be a great but dead rival: Edmund Spenser, Christopher Marlowe or even Dante have been suggested. The answer may well be a composite. Individual living rival candidates include the following, some of whom 'go with' either Southampton or Pembroke.

Barnabe Barnes
George Chapman
Samuel Daniel
John Davies of Hereford
Francis Davison
Michael Drayton
Ben Jonson
Gervase Markham

4: THE DEDICATEE — MR W.H.

Henry Wriothesley, 3rd Earl of Southampton
William Herbert, 3rd Earl of Pembroke
William Shakespeare (S misprinted as H); or William Himself
Sir William Harvey (Southampton's stepfather)
William Hart (an infant nephew)
William Hathaway (perhaps a brother-in-law)
'Willie Hughes' (Oscar Wilde's imaginary boy)

'To be, or not to be – ay, there's the point'

The texts of Shakespeare's plays

The First Folio

In 1623, seven years after Shakespeare's death, his fellow-actors John Heminges and Henry Condell published a collected volume of 36 plays in folio format, known to posterity as the First Folio (F). They categorised the plays as Comedies, Histories and Tragedies. The publication was costly to produce, and also to buy, at 15s. unbound and £1 bound. The large and expensive folio format, in which the printed sheet is folded in half, making two leaves or four sides, was used mainly for big, prestigious publications such as bibles and major historical works. Ben Jonson had published his complete works, including poetry, in 1616, but the publication of the plays of a single author was unprecedented, and is often taken as an indication of the wide respect for and appreciation of Shakespeare's work during and immediately after his lifetime.

Without the publication of the First Folio, half of Shakespeare's plays would have been lost, since it is the only source for 18 texts. The two plays absent from it which are now generally taken as part of the 'standard' body of Shakespeare plays are both works of which Shakespeare was not the sole author – *Pericles*, and *The Two Noble Kinsmen*, which was first published much later, in 1634.

Not numbered in the main count are the lost late play *Cardenio*, which may be the original of *Double Falsehood*, a play published in 1728 by Lewis Theobald, who claimed it as Shakespeare's; *Edward III*, possibly by or partly by Shakespeare and published anonymously in 1596, and his part-scene contribution to the collaboratively authored manuscript of *Sir Thomas More*.

KING HENRY V

Henry V is the culmination of the story of Prince Hal (see *1* and *2 Henry IV*), now king. It may have been the first play performed within the 'wooden O', as the opening Chorus describes it, of the new Globe playhouse. Shakespeare wrote the play at the height of his powers. The Chorus speeches that open each act are bold and thrilling, and the breadth of the action and its wide social range are satisfying and effective.

Encouraged by bishops anxious to deflect the new king's attention from their own coffers, Harry declares his right to the French throne. En route to the French battlefield we re-encounter his former companions Pistol and Bardolph, and Mistress Quickly affectingly describes Falstaff on his deathbed. Captains Fluellen, Gower, Jamy and Macmorris represent the nations of Britain (not yet a 'United Kingdom'). On the night before battle Harry wanders incognito among the soldiers; he discusses with them the justice of the war, and muses on his own responsibilities. The following morning he makes a stirring speech to his heavily outnumbered forces before leading them to victory at Agincourt. In a charmingly suggestive scene he wins the hand of the sparky French princess Katherine.

Mixing high and low, serious and comic, the play investigates heroism not simply as the virtue of a high-born individual but in the context of a broader, more 'naturalistic' social canvas. The scenes that follow the high-flown Chorus passages often deflate their rhetoric, bringing the drama effectively down to earth. Later generations have seen the play as a vehicle for affirming or debating national identity, notably in the Olivier and Branagh film versions.

First recorded performance: traditionally, spring 1599, as the first play performed at the new Globe.

Quartos

Nineteen plays survive as individual publications, printed as small-format quarto (Q) volumes (where the printed sheet is folded in half twice, making four leaves or eight sides), and sold for around 6d., all but one in Shakespeare's lifetime (the 19th, *Othello*, was published in 1622). Of these, 14, including *Othello*, were classed by A.W. Pollard in 1909 as 'Good Quartos'. Good Quarto texts are likely to have been printed from Shakespeare's own manuscript (foul papers) or transcribed 'fair copy'. Pollard categorised seven quarto editions as 'Bad Quartos'. Six of these are abbreviated versions of plays also printed as Good Quartos or in F, and some of them are radically garbled. They may have originated in copies made by actors, either as performing texts or for sale, and are of varying levels of reliability. Two plays, *Hamlet* and *Romeo and Juliet*, appeared both as earlier ('Bad') Quartos (Q1), and later ('Good') ones (Q2). The seventh, *Pericles*, occurs in a quarto which looks as though it may fall into the 'Bad' category, but since it is lacking a parallel 'Good' text, it is hard to be certain.

These quarto texts sometimes vary considerably from the versions later printed in F. In some cases the differences may have arisen from cuts, changes or additions made for later performance by Shakespeare or with his approval. The Q *Othello* is striking for its profanity in comparison with F, which was toned down either to comply with the requirements of the censor or perhaps because of the preference of the copyist or compositor. Scholars suggest that *Hamlet* Q1, which prints a play inferior to and very much shorter than that in Q2 or F (though it includes tantalisingly interesting points), reflects a version of the play staged earlier than the version in F and differing from it in interesting ways, but only poorly recalled in its verbal detail.

Names in *Hamlet*

The major characters in the First Quarto of *Hamlet* are:
Hamlet, Gertred, Corambis [i.e. Polonius], Leartes, Ofelia, Horatio, Rossencraft, Gilderstone and Fortenbrasse. The King, later Claudius (in stage directions only), is unnamed.

---

14 GOOD QUARTOS	18 PLAYS ONLY IN THE FIRST FOLIO
Hamlet	*All's Well That Ends Well*
1 Henry IV	*Antony and Cleopatra*
2 Henry IV	*As You Like It*
King Lear	*The Comedy of Errors*
Love's Labour's Lost	*Coriolanus*
The Merchant of Venice	*Cymbeline*
A Midsummer Night's Dream	*Julius Caesar*
Much Ado About Nothing	*1 Henry VI*
Romeo and Juliet	*Henry VIII*
Othello	*King John*
Richard II	*Macbeth*
Richard III	*Measure for Measure*
Titus Andronicus	*The Taming of the Shrew*
Troilus and Cressida	*The Tempest*
	Timon of Athens
7 BAD QUARTOS	*Twelfth Night*
Hamlet	*The Two Gentlemen of Verona*
Henry V	*The Winter's Tale*
2 Henry VI	
3 Henry VI	**2 OUTSIDERS**
The Merry Wives of Windsor	*Cardenio* (lost)
Romeo and Juliet	*Edward III*
[*Pericles*]	

I QUARTO PUBLISHED AFTER THE FIRST FOLIO

The Two Noble Kinsmen

The print run . . . and the remainder

About 1,000 copies of the First Folio were printed, of which probably 229 survive.

Hamlet's most famous speech
as it appears in the First Quarto of 1603

*Q1 may have been compiled with the help of an actor who had played
Marcellus, the role of which he has the best recollection, and who does not
appear in this scene; his powers of recall are, not surprisingly, variable.
A sigh of relief as he reaches the end is almost audible.*

To be, or not to be – ay, there's the point.
To die, to sleep – is that all? Ay, all.
No, to sleep, to dream– ay, marry, there it goes,
For in that dream of death, when we're awaked
And borne before an everlasting judge
From whence no passenger ever returned –
The undiscovered country, at whose sight
The happy smile and the accursed damned.
But for this, the joyful hope of this,
Who'd bear the scorns and flattery of the world –
Scorned by the right rich, the rich cursed of the poor,
The widow being oppressed, the orphan wronged,
The taste of hunger, or a tyrant's reign,
And thousand more calamities besides –
To grunt and sweat under this weary life
When that he may his full quietus make
With a bare bodkin? Who would this endure,
But for a hope of something after death,
Which puzzles the brain, and doth confound the sense –
Which makes us rather bear those evils we have
Than fly to others that we know not of?
Ay, that – O, this conscience makes cowards of us all.
– Lady, in thy orisons be all my sins remembered.

To be, or not to be – that is the question;
Whether 'tis nobler in the mind to suffer
The slings and arrows of outrageous fortune
Or to take arms against a sea of troubles
And by opposing end them; to die: to sleep –
No more, and by a sleep to say we end
The heartache and the thousand natural shocks
That flesh is heir to: 'tis a consummation
Devoutly to be wished – to die: to sleep –
To sleep, perchance to dream – ay, there's the rub,
For in that sleep of death what dreams may come
When we have shuffled off this mortal coil
Must give us pause: there's the respect
That makes calamity of so long life.
For who would bear the whips and scorns of time,
Th'oppressor's wrong, the proud man's contumely,
The pangs of despised love, the law's delay,
The insolence of office and the spurns
That patient merit of th'unworthy takes,
When he himself might his quietus make
With a bare bodkin. Who would fardels bear
To grunt and sweat under a weary life
But that the dread of something after death
(The undiscovered country from whose bourn
No traveller returns) puzzles the will
And makes us rather bear those ills we have
Than fly to others that we know not of.
Thus conscience does make cowards –
And thus the native hue of resolution
Is sicklied o'er with the pale cast of thought,
And enterprises of great pitch and moment
With this regard their currents turn awry
And lose the name of action. Soft you now,
The fair Ophelia! Nymph, in thy orisons
Be all my sins remembered.

Rhetoric 2: Like and unlike

HENDIADYS

Hendiadys is the pith and marrow of *Hamlet*. It is the term for the pairing, for emphasis, of two words or phrases, often as conjunctions where we would expect one to be subordinated to the other. In its simplest form two nouns will be used where we would normally use a noun and adjective, but the same technique is also applied to longer phrases. The purpose can be oppositional or reinforcing. *Hamlet* is full of them. Frank Kermode identifies, among many, many others, 'Hold it a fashion and a toy in blood' (1.3.6), 'dead waste and middle of the night' (1.2.197), 'my weakness and my melancholy' (2.2.536), 'Angels and ministers of grace defend us!' (1.4.39). George T. Wright notes that on another level they are paralleled by plot and character doublings which contribute to the sense of 'unease and mystery' in the play, to which one might add a sense of obsessive circling round a problem.

OXYMORON

Alongside hendiadys in *Hamlet* are numerous examples of **oxymoron**, the linking of unlikes, or contradiction in terms: 'crafty madness', for example, or 'defeated joy'. As Kermode points out, both are well suited to the duplicitous Claudius, whose speech is full of them. Romeo uses oxymoron to express the inexpressible in love: 'O brawling love, O loving hate, / O anything of nothing first create! / O heavy lightness, serious vanity' (1.1.176–8), and Juliet, hearing that Romeo has killed Tybalt, calls him a 'fiend angelical . . . A damned saint' (3.2.75, 79).

Stage directions 5: *Hamlet*

The First Quarto of *Hamlet* includes vivid stage directions, not found in the Second Quarto or First Folio, which may record an actor's recollection of performance practice.

Enter the Ghost in his night-gown. (11.57)

The Ghost, who has previously appeared in full armour, is appropriately dressed for Gertred and Hamlet's private discussion.

Enter Ofelia playing on a lute, and her hair down, singing. (13.14)

Finding a vicarious existence in Hamlet

Samuel Taylor Coleridge, in 1827, exemplifies the quite common tendency to find aspects of oneself in Hamlet . . .

Hamlet's character is the prevalence of the abstracting and generalising habit over the practical. He does not want courage, skill, will, or opportunity; but every incident sets him thinking; and it is curious, and at the same time strictly natural, that Hamlet, who all the play seems reason itself, should be impelled, at last, by mere accident, to effect his object. I have a smack of Hamlet myself, if I may say so.

. . . as T.S. Eliot recognised in 1922:

Few critics have even admitted that *Hamlet* the play is the primary problem and Hamlet the character only secondary. And Hamlet the character has had an especial temptation for that most dangerous type of critic: the critic with a mind which is naturally of the creative order but which through some weakness in creative power exercises itself in criticism instead. These minds often find in Hamlet a vicarious existence for their own artistic realisation. Such a mind had Goethe who made of Hamlet a Werther; and such had Coleridge who made of Hamlet a Coleridge . . .

Misprints 2: Imogen

The heroine of *Cymbeline* appears in the Folio text as Imogen. The name Innogen, however, appears in one of Shakespeare's sources, Holinshed's *Chronicles*, as that of an ancient British Queen; and it was also the name Shakespeare gave to the silent (or discarded) character of Hero's mother in *Much Ado About Nothing*. Simon Forman, an astrologer and theatregoer who noted his visits to several of Shakespeare's plays in 1611, recorded hearing the name Innogen. The name as it has come down to us is probably a misprint.

Hero's mother, who appears only in two stage directions, may have been abandoned for artistic reasons, or perhaps because there were not enough boy actors available at the time to take all the female roles Shakespeare first had in mind.

KING HENRY VI, PARTS 1, 2 AND 3

These three plays, set during the Wars of the Roses, are rarely performed, and in the theatre have tended to be cut-and-combined, sometimes with Richard III, *which concludes the story. Despite this, they can equally well be performed as they were written – as independent plays. They have been extremely effective onstage either way. They did not appear under their now familiar sequenced titles until the 1623 First Folio, although Parts 2 and 3 survive as Quarto texts. They are given their original titles below.*

Although first in the narrative chronology, 1 Henry VI *may perhaps have been written second or last. Shakespeare's sole authorship of the plays is uncertain: Nashe, Greene and Peele have all been suggested as having a hand in parts 1 and 2, though it is also possible that Shakespeare, at the start of his career, was writing in the styles that surrounded him.*

PART 1: 'HAREY THE VJ'

1589–91

1 Henry VI introduces the king who succeeded to the throne as an infant after the death of his father Henry V, whose funeral opens the play; but Henry VI does not appear until Act 3 – an indication of his reluctance as king and of the uncertainties and struggles over power which run through all three plays. Exciting scenes at the Siege of Orleans involve gunners and scaling ladders, and the dominant figure in the play is Talbot, the 'terror of the French', a brave and charismatic leader who dies in battle, while the English emerge victorious but weakened. Also notable is the character of Joan Puzel (Joan of Arc), no holy maid but a termagant who raises demonic spirits. Meanwhile, at home, in the Temple garden in London, Lancastrians and Yorkists choose red and white roses to indicate their allegiances – the episode that gave the Wars of the Roses their name.

First recorded performance: 3 March 1592, at the Rose, by Lord Strange's Men, recorded in Henslowe's diary as the 'ne[w]' play 'harey the vj'.

PART 2: THE FIRST PART OF THE CONTENTION BETWIXT THE TWO FAMOUS HOUSES OF YORK AND LANCASTER

c. 1590–1

England is heading towards civil war in this darker and more brutal play. France is lost and, in an atmosphere of bickering and betrayal, England begins to lose the rule of law. The nobility argue, scheme, have adulterous affairs and consult witches; people are murdered. With degeneration and loss of control at the top, Jack Cade of Kent heads a blackly comic and violent but ultimately unsuccessful rebellion. Fatally, Henry has no desire to be king, while his rival, the ambitious Richard of York, seems to be heading for victory.

PART 3: THE TRUE TRAGEDY OF RICHARD DUKE OF YORK, WITH THE DEATH OF GOOD KING HENRY THE SIXTH

c. 1591

Power and the promise of the crown pass from one side to another as the Yorkists and Lancastrians kill each other in battles and skirmishes from Towton to Barnet. Pious Henry, fatally lacking the strength of character and will to fight off his enemies, laments his inability to lead a simple life of content, while his wife Margaret engages in battles and diplomacy on behalf of their son. A son unknowingly kills his father, and a father his son, in an encapsulation of the horrors of civil war. Civil strife and an atmosphere of revenge leave the stage open to even darker forces: while Edward of York rejoices in victory, his brother, the unscrupulous Richard who will become Richard III, begins to emerge from the chaos.

❧

Shakespeare's handwriting

Six examples of Shakespeare's signature include three signatures in his will. None of his manuscript copy survives, apart from a contribution, almost certainly by him, to the multiple-authored *Sir Thomas More*. These passages show signs of alteration during the writing process, and confident fluency in the penmanship. They also include the word 'hurly', only found on its own in his work, and some distinctive and unusual spellings, among them: 'scilens' (silence); 'deule' (devil, also found in *Hamlet*); 'elamentes' (elements, also found in *Love's Labour's Lost*) and 'Iarman' (German, also found in *2 Henry IV*).

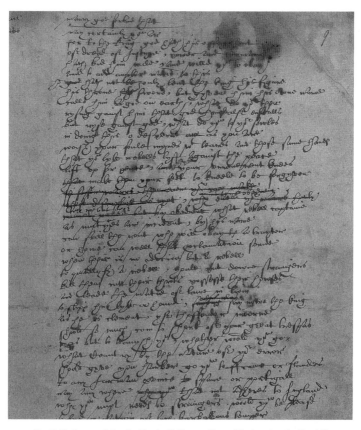

Fig. 10. Shakespeare's handwriting in *Sir Thomas More*, with alterations by 'Hand C'.

KING HENRY VIII

1613

Very different from Shakespeare's history plays of the 1590s, *Henry VIII* eschews battles and violent deaths, and instead presents the rise and fall of individual historical figures, amidst much pageantry. Cardinal Wolsey has organised the Field of the Cloth of Gold, and is at the high point of his career. The Duke of Buckingham, a rival, is condemned for treason. Henry, meanwhile, interested in Anne Bullen (Boleyn), instigates divorce proceedings against the noble Queen Katherine. Publicly, Wolsey tries to persuade Katherine to accept the divorce, but secretly he counsels the Pope against it. His letter to the Pope is discovered, and he bids farewell to his greatness. Anne is crowned queen, and Katherine retires to die. Archbishop Cranmer narrowly escapes imprisonment in the Tower. The birth of the Princess Elizabeth ushers in a golden age.

Historical timings are tweaked to provide a harmonious ending which sheds a glorious light on Elizabeth I and her successor, James, the reigning monarch when the play appeared. Shakespeare wrote it at the end of his career, probably with John Fletcher, with whom he also co-wrote *The Two Noble Kinsmen*.

First recorded performance: Henry VIII is best known for the extra-dramatic event that occurred during a very early performance. On 29 June 1613 a cannon fired at the entrance of the King in Act 1 caught the thatch of the Globe, and the theatre burned to the ground (see p. 41).

❧ *Flowers* ❧

As a boy from a country town, Shakespeare was familiar with hedge-row plants, and often used their country names for pastoral effect. He was also writing at a time when the expansion of exploration meant that large numbers of new plants were arriving in northern Europe and inspiring keen interest. He probably knew the great sixteenth-century illustrated *Herball or General Historie of Plants* by John Gerard, more commonly known as *Gerard's Herball*, first printed in 1597. Poetic passages invoking flowers are some of the most beautiful and poignant in his work, notably in *A Midsummer Night's Dream* and *The Winter's Tale*.

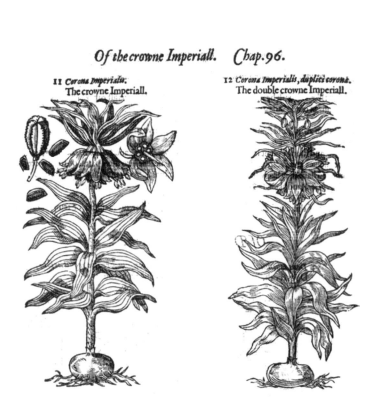

Fig. 11. Crown imperial, from John Gerard's *Herball*, 1597.

For a Shakespearean flower garden

damask roses (the rich red Damascus rose)
musk roses (a scented white rambling rose, then recently introduced)
columbines, carnations
gillyvors (clove-scented pink)
crown-imperial (*fritillaria imperialis*; newly imported from
Constantinople, and all the rage: see opposite page)
flower-de-luce (fleur-de-lis, or iris), lilies 'of all kinds'
a honeysuckle bower
cypress

For a wild-flower garden

daisies, 'faint primroses', daffodils, harebells
'violets dim' (probably the highly scented white violet)
oxlips (the larger cousin of the cowslip)
lark's heels (larkspur), lady-smocks, cuckoo-buds, cuckoo-flowers
crowflowers (either buttercup or ragged robin)
long purples (cuckoo-pint or wild orchid)
golden lads and chimney sweepers (dandelions in flower
and seed, in Warwickshire vernacular)
woodbine (wild honeysuckle), eglantine (wild rose or sweetbrier)
pansies (the small wild pansy, called 'love in idleness')

For a herb garden

rosemary, fennel, wild thyme, rue, mint
lavender, savory, marjoram,
marigold ('mary-buds' – calendula)

Ophelia's flowers

rosemary – 'for remembrance' or a bridegroom (Anne of Cleves
wore rosemary in her bridal crown for Henry VIII)
pansies – 'for thoughts' (*pensées*)
fennel – for flattery
columbines – for deceived lovers
rue, 'herb of grace' – for repentance and forgiveness
daisies – for unrequited love

But no violets – the flower of fidelity.
She garlands herself for death in crowflowers, nettles,
daisies and long purples (4.5.169–78; 4.7.166–9).

Perdita's flowers for middle age

Perdita in *The Winter's Tale* (4.4.103–8) recommends
the 'hot' herbs – lavender, mint, savory, marjoram and marigold,
the 'flowers / Of middle summer' – for 'men of middle age'.

Lear's crown of weeds

King Lear's crown of weeds in his madness (4.4.3–5)
is made with 'rank fumiter (fumitory) and furrow-weeds, /
With burdocks, hemlock, nettles, cuckoo-flowers, / Darnel'.
(The identity of cuckoo-flowers is uncertain;
darnel is an invasive grass.)

🌺 Birds and animals 🌺

The birds . . .

'There is special providence in the fall of a sparrow'

Shakespeare's references to birds are frequent, evocative and full of meaning. They often suggest rural tradition about the significance or behaviour of birds; or they make resonant reference to poetic sources. No doubt sometimes, too, they record his own observation. They appear in some of his most beautiful lines, such as the memorable 'Bare ruined choirs where late the sweet birds sang' (Sonnet 73). Shakespearean birds include:

eagle	nobility, fierceness, high pride: the bird of Jupiter
cormorant	devouring time; war; vanity
crow	blackness, darkness; harshness; ill omen; revenge
raven	blackness; hoarseness; ill omen
falcon, osprey	fierce birds of prey
kite	bloody bird of prey
vulture	devouring bird of prey
owl	night, darkness; ill omen; death
dove	whiteness; mildness, softness; love: the bird of Venus
swan	death; whiteness; softness
lark	tuneful song; morning
nightingale	tuneful song, music; night; love
swallow	swiftness; summer
phoenix	love, mutual and eternal; resurrection
pelican	feeds its young with its own blood: a symbol of Christ
peacock	pride, vanity
cock	strutting masculinity
sparrow	smallness, ordinariness
wren	smallest of birds
chough	a gabbler
parrot	noisy, emptily garrulous
popinjay	(also a parrot) prattler
woodcock	someone easily caught or tricked
(jack)daw	foolishness, empty-headedness
goose	foolish stupidity, garrulousness

As well as
bunting, cuckoo, duck, finch, guinea hen,
hedge sparrow, heron, jay, kestrel, kingfisher, lapwing,
magpie, mallard, martlet, ostrich, paraquito (parrot),
partridge, pheasant, pigeon, quail, rook, seagull, snipe,
starling, thrush, turkey

The ordinary birds of the English countryside appear in the song of the rustic mechanical Bottom (*A Midsummer Night's Dream* 3.1.119–27): the ousel cock (probably the blackbird), throstle (thrush), wren, finch, sparrow, lark and cuckoo. Sometimes the behaviour of birds is closely observed. The dabchick ducks beneath the water under its dialect name 'dive-dapper' in *Venus and Adonis* (86), and Beatrice's friends compare her to a lapwing which 'runs / Close by the ground' (*Much Ado About Nothing* 3.1.24–5). The 'night-owl's lazy flight' is noted (*3 Henry VI* 2.1.129), and Cressida 'fetches her breath as short as a new-ta'en sparrow' (*Troilus and Cressida* 3.2.31–2).

References to birds may mark the time of day. The cock is often used to refer to the hour, most charmingly in *Richard III*, as Northumberland and Surrey are reported walking among their troops to cheer them 'Much about cock-shut time' (5.3.70). It also, of course, symbolises masculine braggadocio: Petruccio promises to be 'A combless cock' if Kate will be his hen (*The Taming of the Shrew* 2.1.228). The crow, in *Macbeth*, flaps off at the coming of night: 'Light thickens; and the crow / Makes wing to th' rooky wood' (3.2.50–1), while the lark conventionally heralds the morning in *A Midsummer Night's Dream*: 'Fairy king, attend and mark: / I do hear the morning lark' (4.1.92–3). The owl is the bird of night, often of ill omen, and the nightingale the bird of night's beauty: 'Except I be by Silvia in the night, / There is no music in the nightingale' (*The Two Gentlemen of Verona* 3.1.178–9).

Other birds have conventional characteristics which would have been familiar to Shakespeare's audience from popular tradition or from illustrated emblems. The raven, crow and eagle (or even the ostrich) are conventionally contrasted with the dove or swan, and the raven also with the lark. The kingfisher, or halcyon, is the symbol of a St Martin's summer, or fine weather late in the year (St Martin's Day is 11 November). The 'martlet' (now a swift, but in Shakespeare's day a house-martin) was supposed to nest only on salubrious buildings; in both *Macbeth* (where it is 'temple-haunting' at 1.6.4) and *The Merchant of Venice* (2.9.28), however, the guest – or foolish martin – is deceived by appearances.

To compare someone to an egg is scornful abuse: 'Finch egg!' (*Troilus and Cressida* 5.1.35); 'thou pigeon-egg of discretion' (*Love's Labour's Lost* 5.1.69); or to a helpless new-hatched nestling: 'This lapwing runs away with the shell on his head' (*Hamlet* 5.2.165–6).

. . . and the bees

So work the honey-bees,
Creatures that by a rule in nature teach
The act of order to a peopled kingdom.
They have a king and officers of sorts,
Where some like magistrates correct at home,
Others like merchants venture trade abroad,
Others like soldiers, armed in their stings,
Make boot upon the summer's velvet buds,
Which pillage they with merry march bring home
To the tent-royal of their emperor,
Who busied in his majesty surveys
The singing masons building roofs of gold.

Henry V 1.2.187–98

Dogs

References to dogs tend to be dismissive. The only notable Shakespearean dog is Crab, of whom his owner, Lance, is very fond.

Nay, I'll be sworn I have sat in the stocks for puddings he hath stolen, otherwise he had been executed.

The Two Gentlemen of Verona 4.4.29–31

Horses

O happy horse, to bear the weight of Antony!
Antony and Cleopatra 1.5.22

When I bestride him, I soar, I am a hawk. He trots the air.
The earth sings when he touches it . . . he is pure air
and fire . . . it is the prince of palfreys.
Henry V 3.7.15–16, 21, 27
(the French Dauphin is pleased with his horse)

He doth nothing but talk of his horse.
The Merchant of Venice 1.2.39–40 (Portia disdains one of her suitors)

Rode he on Barbary?
Richard II 5.5.81 (Richard hears with anguish that
the usurper of his kingdom has even taken his favourite horse)

A horse, a horse, my kingdom for a horse!
Richard III 5.4.7 and 13 (Richard at the battle of Bosworth)

Petruccio and his horse go wooing

Why, Petruccio is coming in a new hat and an old jerkin, a pair
of old breeches thrice-turned; a pair of boots that have been
candle-cases, one buckled, another laced with two broken points;
an old rusty sword ta'en out of the town armoury with a broken
hilt and chapeless; his horse hipped – with an old mothy saddle
and stirrups of no kindred – besides, possessed with the glanders
and like to mose in the chine; troubled with the lampass, infected
with the fashions, full of windgalls, sped with spavins, rayed with
the yellows, past cure of the fives, stark spoiled with the staggers,
begnawn with the bots, weighed in the back and shoulder-shotten,
near-legged before and with a half-cheeked bit and a headstall
of sheep's leather which, being restrained to keep him from
stumbling, hath been often burst and now repaired with knots.
The Taming of the Shrew 3.2.48–58

Cats

*Sadly for cat-lovers, Shakespeare shows no sign of being fond
of cats. In fact the sparse evidence suggests the opposite.*

I could endure anything before but a cat, and now he's a cat to me.
All's Well That Ends Well 4.3.233–4 (Bertram insults Parolles)

I am as vigilant as a cat to steal cream.
1 Henry IV 4.2.57–8 (Falstaff)

I come, Greymalkin!
Macbeth 1.1.8 (the traditional witches' familiar)

Letting 'I dare not' wait upon 'I would',
Like the poor cat i'th' adage.
Macbeth 1.7.44–5

They'll take suggestion as a cat laps milk.
The Tempest 2.1.289

*Shylock alone in Shakespeare speaks up for the
'harmless necessary cat' (The Merchant of Venice* 4.1.55).

Shakespeare pirated

In 1599 William Jaggard published the first edition of 'The Passionate
Pilgrim by W. Shakespeare', a work which contained a few of Shakespeare's sonnets (some of them lifted from *Love's Labour's Lost*, and all
of them probably printed without his permission), and a much larger
number of poems which were in fact by other hands. It was very
successful. Thomas Heywood, two of whose epistles Jaggard published
as Shakespeare's in the third edition, noted in his *Apology for Actors*
that Shakespeare had been 'much offended with M. Jaggard (that
altogether unknown to him) presumed to make so bold with his name'.
Jaggard was later involved in the publication of the First Folio, whether
because he was now a more respectable character or because he still
had an eye for a selling title.

KING JOHN

c. 1590–6

King John's right to the throne is challenged by supporters, headed by Philip, King of France, of his boy nephew Arthur. John's supporters include the Bastard, who claims to be the son of John's dead brother Richard Coeur-de-Lion. The citizens of Angers offer their support to whichever king defeats the other in battle, and are dismayed when the Bastard persuades the two kings to join forces and destroy the town. The citizens only manage to save the day by suggesting marriage between Philip and John's niece. John defies the Pope, whose legate Pandulph excommunicates John and commands Philip to redeclare war. John imprisons Arthur, whose mother Constance laments his loss. He sends Hubert to put out the boy's eyes, but Hubert cannot do it. Later, however, Arthur jumps from the walls of his prison, and dies. John makes peace with the Church, but the English nobles defect to Philip, before suspecting treachery and defecting back again. John is poisoned by a monk and dies; his son Henry becomes king.

The play enthusiastically portrays the pragmatic politics of self-interest. Even the Bastard's illegitimacy is condoned: he is not an out-and-out villain like the later Edmund (*King Lear*) and Don John (*Much Ado*).

KING LEAR

1604–6

Lear, the ageing King of Britain, decides to divide his kingdom between his daughters, while retaining the name of king and a small retinue. Two daughters, Goneril and Regan, declare their love in elaborate flattery; the third, Cordelia, refuses to express her real love in similar terms. Lear disinherits Cordelia. But he is mistaken in the other two, who soon start cutting back his privileges. Enraged and growing mad, Lear vanishes into the storm with his Fool and the faithful Earl of Gloucester. Gloucester is captured by Regan and her husband, who puts out his eyes. Gloucester's son Edgar encounters his blind father as he is making his way to Dover Cliff. Cordelia raises an army to restore Lear, but she and Lear are captured. Meanwhile, Goneril and Regan secretly vie for the affections of Edmund, Gloucester's bastard son, and Goneril tries to persuade him to murder her husband, Albany. She poisons Regan and commits suicide. Albany attempts to restore order, but it is too late; Edmund, fatally wounded by Edgar in a duel, has ordered the murders of Lear and Cordelia. Lear kills Cordelia's murderer but cannot save her. The play ends with Lear grieving over his dead daughter before dying himself.

The story of Lear was popular before Shakespeare picked it up, but he added the significant feature of Lear's madness, as well as the Gloucester subplot. Written after *Hamlet* and *Othello* and before *Macbeth*, for recent audiences the play has become Shakespeare's most powerful tragedy, a work that speaks to a generation that finds itself in a world of bleakness and atrocity.

First recorded performance: 26 December 1606, for James I, at Whitehall.

KING RICHARD II

c. 1595

The first play in the 'second tetralogy' narrates the fall of Richard II and the usurpation of the throne by Bolingbroke, who becomes Henry IV. It presents the deposition of a king, an episode so controversial that it was omitted from editions published during the reign of Elizabeth I.

Capricious, irresponsible and surrounded by favourites, Richard antagonises the nobility of England. He exiles Bolingbroke, son of John of Gaunt, and on the latter's death seizes the family estates. Richard departs to crush rebellion in Ireland, and Bolingbroke returns from exile. In a scene of mocking self-pity, Richard yields to necessity and cedes the throne. Bolingbroke begins to worry about his feckless son Harry; Richard is imprisoned at Pomfret and murdered.

Rhetorical and plangently beautiful, the language marks a poetic advance on the first tetralogy: it makes much use of rhyme and relates the play to its contemporaries, *A Midsummer Night's Dream* and *Romeo and Juliet*. The play includes John of Gaunt's famous lines beginning 'This royal throne of kings', as well as lyrical and unforgettable speeches by Richard which make him a compelling figure, though he is a disaster as a king.

First recorded performance: a revival was commissioned at the Globe by the supporters of the Earl of Essex on 7 February 1601, the eve of the Essex Rebellion.

IV

'The Brightest Heaven of Invention'

Shakespeare the Writer

Playwriting as a career
Shakespeare's contemporaries

Being a professional playwright was a fairly new and somewhat unreliable — even perilous — occupation in the late sixteenth century, though the excitement, with the swift rise of the popular theatres, must have been considerable.

The precarious 1590s

Two highly successful writers died as Shakespeare was starting his career in the early 1590s. *Christopher Marlowe* (1564–93), born the son of a shoemaker in the same year as Shakespeare and educated at Cambridge, went on to write a series of dazzling plays including *Tamburlaine the Great, Doctor Faustus* and *The Jew of Malta.* He died in a tavern brawl in Deptford in 1593. He may have been a spy, removed by a hired killer at a point where he had become a liability. *Thomas Kyd*, who in the late 1580s had written the outstandingly successful *Spanish Tragedy*, was arrested in 1593 on a charge of libelling foreigners. A search of his possessions revealed heretical papers, which he claimed had belonged to Marlowe, with whom he had shared a room in 1591. He died in poverty in 1594, shortly after his imprisonment and torture on these charges. Kyd came from a modest background, but other, university-educated, writers fared no better. Despite having written successful plays, *Robert Greene* (d. 1592), *George Peele* (d. 1596) and *Thomas Nashe* (d. *c.* 1601), all died in reduced circumstances, Greene in a shoemaker's house, 'of a surfeit of pickled herring and rhenish wine'.

> Marlowe . . .
> Had in him those brave translunary things
> That the first poets had, his raptures were
> All air, and fire, which made his verses clear . . .
> *Michael Drayton, 1627*

By the early seventeenth century, things were more stable. Shake-speare's younger contemporary *Ben Jonson* (1572–1637) was luckier, or managed better. Stepson of a bricklayer, he was educated at Westminster School thanks to the generosity of an unknown patron. He wrote prolifically, and with great confidence published his collected *Works* in 1616, the first English playwright ever to do so (and providing a model for the First Folio of Shakespeare). His career had its ups and downs, including his arrest and imprisonment for his part in the notorious play *The Isle of Dogs* in 1597, but he was a survivor: he was awarded a royal pension of 100 marks a year by James I, and although his star waned under Charles I, he remained highly respected. *John Marston* (?1575–1634), an Oxford graduate and lawyer who wrote satires, comedies and tragicomedies, retired from the stage in 1609 to become a priest in Hampshire. *Thomas Middleton* (1580–1627), another bricklayer's son, an Oxford graduate and lawyer, wrote many successful plays, as well as a number of City of London pageants for the Lord Mayor.

Francis Beaumont (*c.* 1585–1616) and *John Fletcher* (1579–1625) formed a successful friendship and writing partnership, though of the 52 plays included in collected editions of 'Beaumont and Fletcher' Beaumont had a hand in less than a quarter, and Fletcher later collaborated more extensively with Philip Massinger. Their writing partnership, however, though brief, remained famous.

Beaumont and Fletcher were the first playwrights of the age to come from the higher reaches of Tudor society. Beaumont, son of a judge, studied at Oxford and began a career as a lawyer, but soon gave up the law to write plays. He wrote both with Fletcher and single-handedly. After a decade in the theatre he made a wealthy marriage and left the profession in about 1613. Fletcher was the son of a Bishop of London, and a Cambridge graduate. Sometime in the early 1600s he began to write with Beaumont, having already produced work of his own, and from about 1611 seems to have been lined up to take over from Shakespeare as principal dramatist with the King's Men, writing three plays in collaboration with him before Shakespeare's retirement. His subsequent career continued successfully and prolifically until his death from plague in 1625.

The nature of the friendship between Beaumont and Fletcher has aroused speculation. Later in the seventeenth century the antiquarian John Aubrey wrote:

They lived together on the Bankside, not far from the Playhouse, both bachelors; lay together; had one wench in the house between them, which they did so admire; the same clothes and cloak, etc. between them.

The 'great reckoning'
Marlowe and Shakespeare

Christopher Marlowe was the brightest star in the firmament when Shakespeare began his career on the London theatrical scene. Born a shoemaker's son in Canterbury in 1564, and thus Shakespeare's exact contemporary, his short life was a far more dramatic one. He went to Corpus Christi College, Cambridge, on a scholarship, and entered some form of government service during his time there – quite possibly as a spy. He was almost certainly homosexual. After leaving Cambridge he became involved in forgery, was imprisoned after taking part in a fight involving a murder, and was accused of heresy. While on bail for this last charge he was killed in a tavern in Deptford, alongside the Thames downriver from London. The man who stabbed him in the eye, Ingram Frizer, claimed that he did so in self-defence in a dispute over the bill. However, all three of Marlowe's companions that day had shady government connections of some kind, and it has been speculated that he was being got out of the way because of his own spying history. He was murdered on 30 May 1593.

At this point in time, Shakespeare's career had barely begun, and had he rather than Marlowe died at Deptford in 1593 we would scarcely remember his name. But amidst all this Marlowe had already written several astonishing plays, box-office triumphs for Philip Henslowe at the Rose theatre. They are bold, amoral, and alight with what he called, in his preface to *Tamburlaine*, 'high astounding terms'. He had an ear for a line unmatched by any of his contemporaries: Jonson admired his 'mighty line'. Looking at Shakespeare's early works, it is hard to avoid the sense that he was trying to emulate and surpass Marlowe in play after play; but it also looks as though the admiration was reciprocal. It is not possible to date either Marlowe's or Shakespeare's early works precisely, but given the date of Marlowe's death, most of Shakespeare's response was posthumous.

Marlowe has been suggested as the 'affable familiar ghost' who nightly haunts Shakespeare in Sonnet 86; the struggle to deal with this ghost seems to have reached its most intense point in the plays written around the turn of the century, and thereafter to have diminished – though it never completely disappeared.

The mutual influences, and the differences (such as Shakespeare's wider tonal range), are more numerous and complex than the comparisons that follow suggest – but they provide a start.

MARLOWE	SHAKESPEARE
Tamburlaine (Parts 1 and 2)	*2, 3 Henry VI*; later, *Henry V* (*Edward III*)
Doctor Faustus	Later, *Macbeth*
The Jew of Malta, the scheming, over-reaching villain	*Titus Andronicus* *Richard III*
Edward II	*Richard II*; plot similarities, and a homosexual king
Dido, Queen of Carthage (with Thomas Nashe)	The player in *Hamlet*, who parodies Marlowe's high bombastic style

The influence of Marlowe is particularly clear in Shakespeare's early work – in the development of his villains, in his plotting, and in some of his rhetoric. Marlowe's poems *Hero and Leander* and *The Passionate Shepherd to his Love* haunt Shakespeare's *Venus and Adonis*. Shakespeare's only straight quotation from a contemporary is from Marlowe, who is the 'dead shepherd' Phoebe quotes, repeating a line from *Hero and Leander* in *As You Like It*:

> Dead shepherd, now I find thy saw of might:
> 'Who ever loved, that loved not at first sight?'
> (3.5.82–3)

Richard II (4.1.281–3) makes close reference to Faustus' 'Was this the face that launched a thousand ships', as does *Troilus and Cressida*, where Helen, more cynically, is 'a pearl / Whose price hath launched above a thousand ships / And turned crowned kings to merchants' (2.2.81–3). *The Merry Wives of Windsor* (3.1.16–25) offers a near-quotation from Marlowe's verses 'Live with me and be my love'. And, again in *As You Like It*, Touchstone (the Fool) says: 'When a man's verses cannot be understood, nor a man's good wit seconded with the forward child, understanding, it strikes a man more dead than a great reckoning in a little room' (3.3.10–13); this recalls both Marlowe's death and his phrase describing the riches of *The Jew of Malta* – 'infinite riches in a little room' (1.37). (Marlowe's provocative phrase itself casts a blasphemous glance at the Virgin Mary carrying the unborn Christ.)

Which of his plots did Shakespeare invent himself?

Along with his contemporaries, Shakespeare relied heavily on earlier literary works for his plots and situations. Even the following plays, which are largely his own creations, contain important elements drawn from other people's works.

Titus Andronicus
Love's Labour's Lost
A Midsummer Night's Dream
The Merry Wives of Windsor
The Tempest

If he tended to use others' stories, he was very skilled at working with them. He would trim a narrative to its core, or complicate and qualify it with one or more subplots – in *Much Ado About Nothing*, for example, the already well-known Hero–Claudio plot strand is balanced with Shakespeare's own invention, the Beatrice–Benedick relationship. Most interestingly to us, he was drawn to find new depth and resonance in an existing plot by exploring interior, psychological rather than exterior, circumstantial motives. This may not extend to minor characters, however, and to a modern audience, valuing character above plot, it sometimes seems as though his interest in the overall plot may have been greater than it was in its nuts and bolts. To us it may seem a major flaw, for example, in *Much Ado About Nothing*, when Margaret fails to reveal Hero's innocence which she has no motive to conceal. Shakespeare briefly acknowledges this problem but it seems not to worry him unduly.

The verbal poetic texture of Shakespeare is the greatest the world has known and is immensely superior to the structure of his plays as plays.
Vladimir Nabokov

KING RICHARD III

c. 1591–3

Set in the thick of the Wars of the Roses, the narrative of *Richard III* takes up the story after the defeat of the Lancastrians in *3 Henry VI*. Richard, Duke of Gloucester, a younger brother of the new Yorkist king, desires the crown for himself. He seduces Lady Anne, daughter-in-law and widow of men he has murdered, and removes all obstacles in his path, including his brother Clarence (stabbed and drowned in a malmsey-butt) and his nephews (the Little Princes in the Tower). He wins the crown, but does not enjoy it for long. At the battle of Bosworth his horse is killed, leaving him, famously, to call for another, and victory goes to the cool-headed Earl of Richmond, the future Henry VII.

The success of this early play was immediate and has never faded. It is largely due to the role of Richard, a bloodthirsty, scheming but charismatic hunchbacked villain, player of many roles – a gift to leading actors. But his is not the only powerful role: in counterpoint to Richard's sardonic wit stands a group of bereaved royal women who are not deceived by events. Led by the terrifying Queen Margaret, widow of Henry VI, they speak their minds.

On 13 March 1602 John Manningham recorded an incident relating to the playwright and his leading actor: see p. 57.

Josephine Tey's 1951 novel *The Daughter of Time* tells the story of a detective who examines the evidence and suggests that Henry VII – a tough and ruthless ruler – had more reason to kill the Princes than did Richard. Although some evidence from Richard's lifetime indicates that he was suspected right from the start, his supporters, from as early as the seventeenth century, have argued that he was framed in a ploy to legitimate the Tudor dynasty. It is certainly the case that his famed deformity was probably invented by an early chronicler.

Shakespeare's reading

When a newcomer to Shakespeare learns that he didn't 'invent his own plots' the discovery can be a shock; it seems like a slur on his achievement. The idea that a true writer or poet relies on native inspiration was central to the Romantic era – though it is detectable earlier – and is still largely current. Originality in the work of Shakespeare and many of his contemporaries is evolutionary rather than revolutionary. They lived in a climate of constant literary influence, cross-fertilisation and glancing quotation. In addition, their education had trained them in analysing and imitating works by classical authors. Their dramatic works were informed by a combination of literary sources, contemporary culture and events (the latter, for political reasons, referred to more often implicitly than directly), and references to other plays in the hugely popular ongoing sequence of theatrical productions. Educated audiences would have shared the playwrights' literary reading and known many of the works referred to, as well as having a similar grounding in classical rhetoric and poetic convention; they would have appreciated the skill with which classical works were referenced. In Tudor music, embellishment and variation on a familiar tune or on a simple bass pattern was very popular; a parallel process is apparent in writing for the stage.

Shakespeare evidently read widely throughout his career; his school education in the classical poets and historians was only a starting point. He would have owned books himself, but would also no doubt have borrowed, and browsed in booksellers' shops (centred round St Paul's). Probably he would have had access to the library of the Earl of Southampton and perhaps those of other patrons or admirers. The many influences on his work include the following chief sources:

The comedies of Plautus

Plautus (c. 254–184 BCE) was the author of Roman comedies whose stock characters, tricksters, and plots of mistaken identity and long-lost relations provide plot-lines and inspiration for *All's Well That Ends Well*, *The Comedy of Errors*, *The Taming of the Shrew* and *Twelfth Night*.

LOVE'S LABOUR'S LOST

c. 1594–5

The King of Navarre persuades three of his lords to study for three years and forswear the company of women during that time. However, when the Princess of France arrives at his court to claim a portion of Aquitaine, with a party including three ladies, the lords are very taken by the ladies, as is the King by the Princess, and the play follows their courtships through letters, poems, concealments and masquerade, all set in a dazzling sequence of puns, rhymes and sonnets. Love's labour is lost at the end of the play when, following news of the death of the Princess's father, the women refuse to give the men an answer until a year and a day have passed.

A set of comic characters in the *commedia dell'arte* style is presented in counterpoint: they include a fantastical Spaniard and a country couple, a schoolmaster, a priest and the constable, Dull. The acerbically witty leading pair, Berowne and Rosaline, are forerunners of *Much Ado*'s Beatrice and Benedick, but the language of all the characters is scintillating and playful, to a degree that can make the play difficult for modern audiences.

The 1598 First Quarto of *Love's Labour's Lost* is the first surviving printed play acknowledging 'W. Shakespeare' as its author on the title-page.

First recorded performances: 'this last Christmas' 1597, for Queen Elizabeth; and Christmas 1604, for Henry Wriothesley, 3rd Earl of Southampton, to entertain James I; Southampton had been imprisoned for his part in the Essex Rebellion, and was released on the accession of the new king.

The poetry of Ovid

Shakespeare would have studied the poetry of the Roman poet Ovid (43 BCE–17 CE) in depth at school, in Latin, learning how to analyse and emulate his grammar and poetical rhetoric. He was also very familiar with Arthur Golding's translations of Ovid's work, dating from the 1560s. Ovid clearly remained a lifelong object of admiration and source of inspiration. He is a huge influence on Shakespeare's work stylistically and conceptually, and lies behind many of his references to classical mythology. In particular, his famous *Metamorphoses* are a major source for *Venus and Adonis* and *The Rape of Lucrece*. Plays notably deriving elements from Ovid are *A Midsummer Night's Dream* and *Titus Andronicus* at the beginning of his career and the late comedies at the end of it, though the influence is detectable throughout. Ovid is several times referred to by name in the plays. Golding was connected with the family of the Earl of Oxford, and the Ovidian influence is cited in support of the Oxfordian authorship claim.

The tragedies of Seneca

Senaca, a Roman Stoic philosopher of the first century CE, was tutor to Nero, and was famously obliged to commit suicide because of his part in an alleged conspiracy against the Emperor. He was also a writer of blood-spattered sensational tragedies. His rhetoric was much admired by the Elizabethans, and the influential revenge play *The Spanish Tragedy* by Thomas Kyd brought gory and ghost-ridden Senecan revenge into high fashion. Seneca the philosopher can be traced in *Julius Caesar* and *The Tempest*, and Seneca the tragedian in *Titus Andronicus*, *Richard III*, *Hamlet* and *Macbeth* in particular.

Sir Thomas North's translation of Plutarch's
LIVES OF THE NOBLE GRECIANS AND ROMANS, 1579

Plutarch, a Greek historian of the first and second centuries CE, was enduringly popular thanks to his lively narrative style. He was widely read in the translation (made from a French version by Jacques Amyot) by North, a soldier who later served in Ireland and against the

Spanish. Shakespeare drew on North for *Antony and Cleopatra*, *Corio-lanus*, *Julius Caesar*, *A Midsummer Night's Dream* and *Timon of Athens*.

An alchemical transformation

From Sir Thomas North's translation of Plutarch's *Lives of the Noble Grecians and Romans* (*Life of Marcus Antonius*), 1579

She disdained to set forward otherwise, but to take her barge in the river of Cydnus, the poope whereof was of gold, the sailes of purple, and the owers of silver, which kept stroke in rowing after the sounde of the musicke of flutes, howboyes, citherns, violls, and such other instruments as they played upon in the barge. And now for the person of her selfe: she was layed under a pavillion of cloth of gold of tissue, apparelled and attired like the goddesse Venus, commonly drawen in picture: and hard by her, on either hand of her, pretie faire boyes apparelled as painters doe set forth god Cupide, with litle fannes in their hands, with the which they fanned wind upon her.

From *Antony and Cleopatra* (2.2.201–15)

> The barge she sat in, like a burnished throne,
> Burned on the water; the poop was beaten gold;
> Purple the sails, and so perfumed that
> The winds were love-sick with them; the oars were silver,
> Which to the tune of flutes kept stroke, and made
> The water which they beat to follow faster,
> As amorous of their strokes. For her own person,
> It beggared all description: she did lie
> In her pavilion, cloth-of-gold of tissue,
> O'erpicturing that Venus where we see
> The fancy outwork nature. On each side her
> Stood pretty dimpled boys, like smiling cupids,
> With divers-coloured fans, whose wind did seem
> To glow the delicate cheeks which they did cool,
> And what they undid did.

Raphael Holinshed and others

Holinshed, a translator, was given this vast historical project by his employer, the printer/publisher Reginald Wolfe. Shakespeare relied heavily on his work throughout the history plays, and in *Cymbeline, King Lear* and *Macbeth*.

The Bible

Shakespeare's work is infused with knowledge of, allusion to and quotation from the Bible. Thanks to the rise in Protestantism, the Bible was now available in several translations. Study of Shakespeare's close quotation suggests that he was most familiar with the Geneva Bible of 1560.* This had been produced by Protestants exiled by Mary and established in Calvinist Switzerland. The translation was derived from Greek New Testament and Hebrew Old Testament sources, and was largely based on the earlier fine translations by William Tyndale and Myles Coverdale. Shakespeare evidently also used other versions, and was aware of controversies over rival translations.

Connections can be found in his work to 42 books of the Bible. The language and content of the Bible is treated with close knowledge and with respect, though it is also frequently used ironically for effect.

Other sources include . . .

Boccaccio's fourteenth-century *Decameron* (*All's Well That Ends Well, Cymbeline*) and other collections of Italian romances, at least one of which, the *Hecatommithi*, was only available in Italian.

The works of many English writers, particularly Geoffrey Chaucer, Sir Philip Sidney (especially the sonnets and the *Arcadia*), Edmund Spenser (the sonnets and *The Faerie Queene*), and his contemporaries Christopher Marlowe, Robert Greene and John Lyly.

---

* The Geneva Bible was also known as the *Breeches Bible*, after a passage in Genesis 3.7 referring to Adam and Eve: 'Then the eyes of them both were opened, and they knew that they were naked, and they sewed fig tree leaves together, and made themselves breeches.' The later King James version prefers the more modest word 'aprons'.

The *Essais* of Montaigne, published in an English translation by John Florio in 1603. Montaigne, a French contemporary of Shakespeare, invented the term *essai* ('trial'). His influence has been detected in Hamlet's philosophising and questioning, and can be found in a number of other later plays, most clearly in *The Tempest.* Florio's connection with the Earl of Southampton is adduced to the argument for Southampton being the 'fair youth' of the sonnets.

A number of historical writers and texts such as *The Mirror for Magistrates* (a popular history series, source for a number of the history plays and for *Cymbeline* and *King Lear*), and a courtesy book, Castiglione's *Book of the Courtier* (in translation).

Not all by Shakespeare?
Collaboration and revision

The 'canon' of accepted 'official' Shakespeare plays is based on those printed in the First Folio, with the addition of *Pericles* and, increasingly, *The Two Noble Kinsmen*. Shakespeare probably made a contribution to *Sir Thomas More*, and he has been proposed as author or part author of *Edward III*.

But even within this list, all is not as it might seem. It has been estimated that nearly half of all plays written for the public stage during this period were co-authored – perhaps to speed up production – and on a very pragmatic basis. Different acts and scenes were apportioned to each contributor, sometimes on the basis of their skills at different kinds of writing – comic or highly serious, for example. In some cases it is clear that not much discussion went on. Shakespeare and Fletcher, collaborating on *The Two Noble Kinsmen*, seem to have been working from different sources, and used different spellings and scansion for the name of one of the characters. Evidence for collaboration derives from title-pages or entries in the Stationers' Register, or from within the plays themselves. In other cases plays were probably revised after their first performances.

Co-authored with

THOMAS MIDDLETON
Macbeth (additions/revision?), *Measure for Measure* (revision?)
Timon of Athens

JOHN FLETCHER
Cardenio (a lost late play, possibly *Double Falsehood*)
Henry VIII, The Two Noble Kinsmen

GEORGE WILKINS
Pericles

ANTHONY MUNDAY, HENRY CHETTLE,
THOMAS DEKKER, THOMAS HEYWOOD AND 'HAND C'
Sir Thomas More

UNIDENTIFIED
3 Henry VI

PROBABLY GEORGE PEELE
Edward III (?)
Titus Andronicus

POSSIBLY THOMAS NASHE OR
ANOTHER UNIDENTIFIED CO-AUTHOR
1 Henry VI

The power of Shakespeare's name remains, however: the plays have not generally been published with more than his name alone on the spine or title-page.

With additional contributions by . . .
Actors recollecting text-in-performance for Quarto editions
(the actor playing Marcellus in *Hamlet* is an example)
Anyone who wrote out a prompt-book (a likely source of *Macbeth*)
Fair-copyists (printing-house scribes)
Compositors (typesetters)
Censors

MACBETH

c. 1606

The Scottish thane Macbeth – encouraged by the prophecies of three witches on the heath to aim for the throne, and urged on by his wife – murders King Duncan and arranges the assassination of his prophesied rival, the noble Banquo. He is haunted by a spectral dagger and by Banquo's ghost. The wife and child of his enemy Macduff are mercilessly slaughtered, and the nobles rise up against his increasingly tyrannical rule. Lady Macbeth, tormented by guilt, sleepwalks and tries to wash her hands of blood. The witches' prophecies prove equivocal, and Macbeth is overthrown in battle; Duncan's son Malcolm becomes king.

The play pays homage to the interests of Shakespeare's company's patron – King James had written a study of witchcraft, and was a descendent of Banquo, who is presented far more favourably here than in the sources. It also reflects the treasonous Gunpowder Plot of 1605. Its brevity and stylistic variation suggest that the surviving First Folio text may be an adaptation for later performance, with additions, by Middleton.

Dark, intense, brief and rough-versed, *Macbeth* lends itself to psychologically focused interpretation. It is supposed to be an unlucky play, and superstition notoriously declares that it should never be named in the theatre.

First recorded performance: 20 April 1611, at the Globe, recorded in his commonplace book by Simon Forman.

> When you're a young man, Macbeth is a character part. When you're older, it's a straight part.   *Laurence Olivier*

Ralph Crane

One copyist about whom quite a lot can be deduced is Ralph Crane. Crane was a lawyer's clerk who took up dramatic copying late in life, and worked on a number of plays for the First Folio. He applied his own favourite kinds of punctuation – in particular, colons, parentheses, hyphens, and apostrophes for words such as *do'st* for *doest*. He seems also to have elaborated the character listings with his own descriptions, and to have been fond of lengthy stage directions, often listing all the characters who were to appear in a scene at the beginning of it, whether they entered at that point or later. His fuller stage directions may have been intended as a help to those reading a printed page rather than viewing a play, and possibly recall productions he attended himself.

His input begins to resemble what we might now expect from a publisher's copy-editor. Ernst Honigmann, looking at his work on *Othello*, describes him in terms which many authors might use of their editors: 'Crane was neither humble nor faithful; he "improved" his transcripts, as he would see it, a creative or destructive role, depending on one's point of view.'

Not by Shakespeare at all?

Shakespeare's popularity made his name a major selling point. A number of plays published as his in the early seventeenth century are undoubtedly not his at all. Others were variously attributed to him in the course of the century by hopeful printers and booksellers, and others again ascribed to him from the eighteenth century onwards by equally hopeful editors and scholars. Chief amongst these apocryphal plays are

Arden of Faversham
Double Falsehood
Edmund Ironside
Edward III
Fair Em
Locrine
The London Prodigal
Mucedorus
Thomas, Lord Cromwell
The Troublesome Reign of King John

The Birth of Merlin – William Rowley
The Puritan – Thomas Middleton
Sir John Oldcastle – Michael Drayton, Anthony Munday,
Richard Hathway and Robert Wilson
A Yorkshire Tragedy – Thomas Middleton

Only *Edward III*, printed in 1596, has lasted the course as a serious and long-standing contender for genuine part-Shakespearean authorship. The distinguished eighteenth-century editor Edward Capell and Alfred, Lord Tennyson in the nineteenth century, as well as a number of recent scholars, have argued the case for his having a hand in the play. *Double Falsehood* has recently been championed once again as drawn from the lost *Cardenio*.

A play by any other name

Love's Labour's Won
(either a lost play, or another name for *Much Ado About Nothing*)
The First Part of the Contention (2 Henry VI)
The True Tragedy of Richard Duke of York (3 Henry VI)
Twelfth Night or What You Will
All Is True (Henry VIII)

Five guys named Antonio

- The 'Merchant of Venice', whose life is endangered when he borrows money from Shylock to give to his friend Bassanio, who wants to marry Portia. Antonio relies on his trading ships returning safely, and risks forfeiting a pound of flesh if they fail.

- Loyal uncle to Hero in *Much Ado About Nothing*.

- Brother to Prospero and usurper of his dukedom in *The Tempest*. He is shipwrecked on Prospero's island and the dukedom is eventually restored.

- A sea captain in *Twelfth Night*.

- Father to Proteus, one of the *Two Gentlemen of Verona*.

❧ *Food* ❧

Food and drink for Shakespeare's characters is a homely, everyday business. They talk of beef, hare and partridge, of pies, apples ('leather-coats' in *2 Henry IV* 5.3.40) and cheese, and of sack (*vin sec*, or dry wine, to which, however, sugar was added) and ale.

Sir Andrew Aguecheek is fond of beef, though he thinks it does harm to his wit (*Twelfth Night* 1.3.84–5), and Petruccio declares that burnt meat is a sign of choler (*The Taming of the Shrew* 4.1.159–61). Hal's laddish companion Poins likes conger (eel) and fennel – still a combination appreciated by food writers (*2 Henry IV* 2.4.245).

TO BOILE EELS

Recipe from Thomas Dawson, The Good huswifes Iewell, *printed near St Paul's in 1596*:

. . . boyle with a little faire water and vineger, a little salt, and bayleaves, and sauce them in vineger, and a little of the broth that they are sodden in with a little salt, and as you see cause shift your sauce, as you do beefe in brine . . . and let it be cold, and serve it foorth with vineger, and a little fennel upon it but first or yee seeth it, it must be watered.

Evans in *The Merry Wives of Windsor* looks forward to the conclusion of his dinner – 'there's pippins and cheese to come' (1.2.12) – and a shepherd's son in *The Winter's Tale* goes over his shopping list for a celebration:

I must have saffron to colour the warden pies; mace; dates, none – that's out of my note; nutmegs, seven; a race or two of ginger – but that I may beg; four pound of prunes, and as many of raisins o'th' sun. (4.3.45–8)

The Warden, or Worcester Black Pear, a good baking pear, is recorded at Warden Abbey in Bedfordshire in the thirteenth century; it is also supposed to have appeared in the crest of Worcester bowmen at the battle of Agincourt in 1415.

On a more sociological note, Mistress Elbow, 'great with child', is declared – 'saving your honours' reverence' – to have a longing for stewed prunes, the standard offering in brothels, where the sale of bread, ale and meat was forbidden by law in order to discourage custom (*Measure for Measure* 2.1.87–8).

Straightforward enjoyment of food and drink seems to be associated by Shakespeare with happier, pre-Puritan days. 'If sack and sugar be a fault, God help the wicked', says Falstaff to Hal in *1 Henry IV* (2.4.464–5), and Toby Belch, a good trencherman, famously asks, 'Dost thou think because thou art virtuous, there shall be no more cakes and ale?' (*Twelfth Night* 2.3.113–14).

Perhaps, though, food was not particularly important to him – there are no overt scenes of gluttony, and a couple of mentions of excess in *Antony and Cleopatra*, where Maecenas questions Enobarbus in disbelief – 'Eight wild boars roasted whole at a breakfast, and but twelve persons there. Is this true?' (2.2.189–90).

✌ *Two frocks* ✌

Margaret describes 'the Duchess of Milan's gown that they praise so' to Hero, who is planning her wedding:

> By my troth, 's but a night-gown in respect of yours – cloth o'gold, and cuts, and laced with silver, set with pearls, down sleeves, side sleeves and skirts round underborne with a bluish tinsel. But for a fine, quaint, graceful and excellent fashion, yours is worth ten on't.
>
> *Much Ado About Nothing* 3.4.17–21

And Petruccio disparages the dress proposed by a tailor for his bride Kate:

> What's this? A sleeve? 'Tis like a demi-cannon.
> What, up and down carved like an apple-tart?
> Here's snip, and nip, and cut, and slish and slash,
> Like to a cithern in a barber's shop.
> Why, what i'devil's name, tailor, call'st thou this?
>
> *The Taming of the Shrew* 4.3.90–4

MEASURE FOR MEASURE

c. 1604

The Duke of Vienna leaves his deputy Angelo in charge of the city, but returns disguised as a friar to observe events. Claudio has got his fiancée pregnant, and Angelo condemns him to death under an old law. He also orders that the brothels in the suburbs be demolished. Claudio's sister Isabella, about to become a nun, is persuaded to plead for his life. Her chaste eloquence inflames the chilly Angelo, who offers to save Claudio if Isabella will yield him her virginity; Claudio begs her to sacrifice herself on his behalf, but she is shocked at the suggestion. The Duke now begins a series of machinations. Angelo is tricked into sleeping with his former fiancée Mariana, thinking she is Isabella. He breaks his word and orders Claudio's execution, but the Duke sends him the head of another prisoner. Returning as himself, the Duke arranges for the truth to be revealed. Having obliged Angelo to marry Mariana and spared his life at Isabella's pleading, he asks Isabella to marry him, but the play gives her no response.

This late, dark comedy takes place in claustrophobic settings – a convent, a prison, a brothel and a moated grange. In the complex character of the Duke it reflects the new King James's interest in the responsibilities of rulers.

First recorded performance: 26 December 1604, St Stephen's Night, 'Mesur for Mesur' by 'Shaxberd', at Whitehall.

THE MERCHANT OF VENICE

1596-7

Bassanio, a young Venetian short of money, wishes to woo the heiress Portia, and is persuaded by his merchant friend Antonio to borrow 3,000 ducats from the Jewish moneylender Shylock. Shylock, whom Antonio has often insulted, offers the loan without interest, proposing as if jestingly that the surety be a pound of Antonio's flesh.

Portia must accept the suitor who chooses the right one of three caskets. Proud princes choose gold and silver, but Bassanio correctly picks the lead casket. Shylock's daughter Jessica elopes with Lorenzo, taking many of Shylock's valuables. Antonio's ships are reported lost and Shylock goes before the Duke to demand his price, refusing the return of the ducats, which Portia has offered. A young lawyer 'Balthazar' defends Antonio; he is Portia, disguised. She presses Shylock to the limit, and he sharpens his knife for his pound of flesh. At the last moment Portia declares that the bond allows not a drop of blood to be shed. Shylock is stripped of his estate and forced to convert. Portia and her maid reveal their identities to their new husbands and Antonio's ships are reported safe.

The enduringly problematic question of how far the play is sympathetic to Shylock has only been rendered more painful by the persecution of the Jews under the Nazis. Shylock is unlikeable and vindictive; but like Malvolio, he is also 'most notoriously abused', and his famous speeches invite sympathy, calling for an acknowledgment of common humanity. Ultimately, however, the play presents his punishment and humiliation as the 'right' conclusion.

First recorded performances: 10 February 1605, Shrove Sunday, by the King's Men for James I, at court, and again on the following Tuesday.

THE MERRY WIVES OF WINDSOR

probably 1597

This enduringly popular and very English play was supposedly written at the request of Queen Elizabeth, who according to tradition wished to see Falstaff in love. It is Shakespeare's only comedy set in England (discounting the Induction to *The Taming of the Shrew* and the tragicomic ancient British *Cymbeline*), and is firmly located amidst the provincial middle class.

Sir John Falstaff decides to better his fortunes by seducing Mistress Page and Mistress Ford. Comparing the letters he sends them, they decide to lead him on and at the same time tease the causelessly jealous Master Ford, and arrange a rendezvous via Mistress Quickly. Ford is warned, and visits Falstaff in the guise of a rival would-be lover. Falstaff twice visits Mistress Ford and twice escapes discovery, by hiding in a laundry basket and by dressing as an old woman. Meanwhile, the Pages' daughter Anne prefers the gentlemanly Fenton to the better-off candidates her father favours. At Falstaff's final rendezvous in Windsor Park he is teased by the company dressed as fairies, until all is revealed.

Fast-moving and farcical, the play pursues various subplots through swift twists and turns. The final scene, though, has some of the woodland magic of *A Midsummer Night's Dream*.

Ten worst villains

IAGO
a jealous, lascivious, manipulative, amoral and affectless murderer

AARON
*murder; instigates rape and mutilation
(cutting off hands and tongue to conceal evidence)*

CLAUDIUS
*guilty of fratricide and regicide, posthumous incest,
attempted murder of his nephew*

RICHARD III
*commissions political murders in and beyond
his own family, including children; seduces widow
whose husband and father he killed*

MACBETH
regicide; murder, including children

GONERIL
*murders sister; daughterly cruelty and unsisterly
behaviour; adultery*

REGAN
*murder; accessory to putting out of eyes; daughterly cruelty
and unsisterly behaviour; adultery*

LADY MACBETH
incitement to murder; planting false evidence

EDMUND
*brotherly betrayal; affairs with two married sisters at once;
filial disrespect*

DON JOHN
malicious slander; brotherly hate

V

'The Two-hours' Traffic of Our Stage'

Facts and Figures

Stage directions 6: Action

Exeunt omnes, as fast as may be, frighted.
The Comedy of Errors 4.4.149

Enter the Prince marching, with Peto, and Falstaff meets
him, playing on his Truncheon like a Fife.
1 Henry IV 3.3.87

Here Gloucester's men beat out the Cardinal's men, and
enter in the hurly-burly the Mayor of London, and his
officers.   *1 Henry VI* 1.3.56

A noise within, Down with the Tawny-Coats . . .
A noise again, Stones, Stones . . .
Enter in skirmish with bloody pates.
1 Henry VI 3.1.73, 75, 85

Enter Juliet somewhat fast, and embraceth Romeo.
Romeo and Juliet 2.6.15

Cornets in sundry places. Noise and hallowing as people a
Maying. Enter Arcite alone.
The Two Noble Kinsmen 3.1

And, most famous of all . . .

Exit, pursued by a bear.
The Winter's Tale 3.3.57 – a sad end for Antigonus

Longest and shortest plays

Assessed by word count, the five longest evenings
on the Shakespeare stage are:

Hamlet	29,551
Richard III	28,309
Cymbeline	26,778
Coriolanus	26,579
Othello	25,887

And the five shortest:

The Comedy of Errors	14,369
The Tempest	16,036
A Midsummer Night's Dream	16,087
Macbeth	16,436
The Two Gentlemen of Verona	16,883

Because Folio and Quarto texts differ where both survive, it is not always possible to give a definitive length for a play. The number of prose lines also, of course, varies according to the book's size and page design. However, *Hamlet* is unarguably the longest play (though the Quarto and Folio versions differ by several hundred lines), estimated by the editors of the Pelican Shakespeare at 3,776 lines, and by Marvin Spevack, in his magisterial *Complete and Systematic Concordance to the Works of Shakespeare*, at 29,551 words. *The Comedy of Errors* is the shortest, with, by Pelican's count, 1,756 lines, and by Spevack's, 14,369 words. *Macbeth* is an exceptionally short tragedy. The rankings above are by Spevack's word count.

Hamlet and *Richard III*, as well as being long, include the two longest roles, those of Hamlet and Richard.

The Prologue to *Romeo and Juliet* refers to 'the two-hours' traffic of our stage' (12), although Theseus, in *A Midsummer Night's Dream* (5.1. 32–4), written at around the same time, asks the assembled company a question that suggests a longer expected time for entertainment:

> Come now; what masques, what dances shall we have,
> To wear away this long age of three hours
> Between our after-supper and bed-time?

Longest and shortest roles

Again, because of differences between source texts, it is not possible to provide a definitive length for all roles. However, Marvin Spevack's *Concordance* provides word counts by role (as well as much other fascinating material) for plays in the Folio. Hamlet is the most substantial part, by some margin, and the longest female role is that of Rosalind in *As You Like It*; she is followed by Cleopatra, Portia, Imogen and Juliet. The longest clown's roles were both written for Robert Armin: Feste in *Twelfth Night* and Touchstone in *As You Like It*.

The *Concordance* gives the following role-lengths in number of words.

First eleven

Hamlet	11,563
Richard III	8,826
Iago (*Othello*)	8,434
Henry V	8,338
The Duke (*Measure for Measure*)	6,536
Coriolanus	6,434
Timon of Athens	6,325
Othello	6,237
Richard II	5,987
Antony (*Antony and Cleopatra*)	5,949
Rosalind (*As You Like It*)	5,698

Second eleven

Titus Andronicus	5,670
King Lear	5,592
Falstaff (*1 Henry IV*)	5,517
Falstaff (*2 Henry IV*)	5,449
Brutus (*Julius Caesar*)	5,394
Macbeth	5,291
Leontes (*The Winter's Tale*)	4,874
Berowne (*Love's Labour's Lost*)	4,809
Prospero (*The Tempest*)	4,700
Cleopatra	4,686
Romeo	4,677

Hamlet also dominates his play, speaking 39.1% of it (by word count). Timon of Athens speaks 35.6% and both Iago and Henry V 32.6%.

Famous partnerships

Romeo (19.6%)	4,677	4,271	Juliet (17.9%)
Antony (25.1%)	5,949	4,686	Cleopatra (19.7%)
Benedick (18%)	3,738	2,359	Beatrice (11.4%)
Petruccio (22.5%)	4,605	1,759	Kate (8.6%)
Macbeth (32.2%)	5,291	1,901	Lady Macbeth (11.6%)
Rosalind (26.7%)	5,698	2,378	Orlando (11.1%)

Juliet and Romeo are the only well-matched couple here, each speaking a little under 20% of the text. Beatrice may seem as wordy as Benedick in performance, but in fact he is the dominating talker, even in the scenes they share. (Hero, the second heroine in *Much Ado About Nothing*, is modestly retiring, speaking only 980 lines.) Orlando hardly gets a word in edgeways with Rosalind. Kate's part in *The Taming of the Shrew* is very small, and almost a quarter of it is contained within a single speech – her oration on wifely duty at the end of the play. Size isn't everything, though; Lady Macbeth's role is surprisingly small on paper, but very powerful on stage.

The balance of power

Falstaff (*2 HIV*) (21.2%)	5,449	2,442	Hal (9.5%)
Iago (32.6%)	8,434	6,237	Othello (24.1%)
Richard II (27.5%)	5,987	3,119	Bolingbroke (14.3%)

Richard II and Falstaff may lose the power struggles, but they win the battles for our ears.

Portia (22%)	4,605
Shylock (13.7%)	2,876
Bassanio (12.4%)	2,590
The Duke (30.7%)	6,536
Isabella (14.2%)	3,010
Angelo (11.1%)	2,371

Four lovers

Helena	11.2%	7.9%	Hermia
Demetrius	6.6%	8.7%	Lysander

Shortest speaking role

The shortest named speaking role is that of the general Taurus in *Antony and Cleopatra*, who at 3.8.2 utters the two words: 'My lord?'

Verse ...

About 75% of the writing in the plays overall is verse. *Richard II* and *King John* (also *Edward III*, possibly by or partly by Shakespeare) contain no prose at all, and 1 and 3 *Henry VI* less than 1%. Less than 10% of *The Merry Wives of Windsor* is in blank verse (3.8% is in rhymed verse).

Shakespeare rhymes more often in the plays of the early 1590s, his early plays for the Chamberlain's Men, which are obsessively fascinated by language. Almost half of both *A Midsummer Night's Dream* and *Love's Labour's Lost* is rhymed, about a fifth of *Richard II* (many of the rhyming lines being Richard's), and 16.6% of *Romeo and Juliet* – a surprisingly high proportion for a tragedy; though this is a 'tragedy' that plays around with the comic and tragic genres.

... and prose

The proportions of prose and verse vary widely through the plays, and though the comedies tend to contain more prose and the histories less, the story is not a simple one. Whole scenes may be set in either one or the other, or the writing may move flexibly between the two. Prose can be there for particular effect – as it is in the trial scene in *The Merchant of Venice*, where the letter of recommendation introducing Portia as a young lawyer is the only prose passage in a verse scene. Prose in Shakespeare is not just the medium for comic and working-class characters: some of his most dazzling speakers are equally potent, or even at their best, in prose – Falstaff, Hal and Hamlet, for example. Characters across the social range in *Much Ado About Nothing* (about 70% prose, according to the Pelican Shakespeare) speak in a range of styles from the demotic to that of the educated elite.

Top five plays for prose

The Merry Wives of Windsor	86.6%
Much Ado About Nothing	71.7%
Twelfth Night	61.3%
As You Like It	54.5%
2 Henry IV	48.7%

Most and fewest characters

Not surprisingly, the English histories are the most heavily populated plays, with 40 or 50 speaking roles and other walk-on parts. *Richard III* has over 50 speaking roles, not counting walk-on guards, halberdiers, gentlemen, lords, citizens, attendants and soldiers. Many of the roles would have been doubled. The comedies are lighter on their feet, generally with around 20 characters; *The Comedy of Errors* and *Love's Labour's Lost* both have fewer than 20 speaking roles. *Othello*, with 19 speaking parts (not counting the odd messenger), has the sparsest cast list amongst the tragedies; this is surely appropriate to its largely domestic setting and contributes to the play's sense of claustrophobia.

There are far fewer female than male roles. Boy actors' careers were brief, and no doubt it would have been exceptional to have more than a couple of very good actors available at any one time. *Macbeth* and *Pericles* have seven female roles each; otherwise the norm is three to five, and *Hamlet, Julius Caesar* and *Timon of Athens* only have two.

Nasty deaths

EATEN BY A BEAR
Antigonus, *The Winter's Tale*

DROWNED IN A MALMSEY-BUTT
The Duke of Clarence, *Richard III*

BURNED AT THE STAKE
Joan Puzel (Joan of Arc), *1 Henry VI*

KILLED AND SERVED TO THEIR MOTHER IN A PIE
Chiron and Demetrius, sons of Tamora, *Titus Andronicus*

ASPHYXIATED BY HER HUSBAND
Desdemona, *Othello*

BETRAYED BY A FRIEND
Julius Caesar, stabbed by his friend Brutus
and
Rosencrantz and Guildenstern,
killed after Hamlet transferred to them the death
warrant intended for himself

STABBED THROUGH A CURTAIN AT A VENTURE
Polonius, *Hamlet*

ONSTAGE MURDER OF A CHILD
Prince Edward (*3 Henry VI*) and Lady Macduff's son (*Macbeth*),
both murdered in the presence of their mothers

Stage directions 7: *Othello*

Many of the stage directions in *Othello* establish an intimate and
domestic atmosphere; a number of them mention lights and torches:

Enter Brabantio in his night gown, and servants with Torches. (Q; 1.1.157)
Enter Othello with a light. (Q) *Enter Othello, and Desdemona in her bed.*
(F; 5.2.0)

Oth. falls on the bed. (Q; 5.2.195)

A MIDSUMMER NIGHT'S DREAM

c. 1594–6

Set in a wood near Athens, and framed in the court of Theseus and his Amazonian queen Hippolyta, this beautiful and satisfying comedy nonetheless feels deeply English. Helena, Hermia, Lysander and Demetrius, young and in a tangle of relationships, wander in the wood, while in another part of the forest a group of working men – 'mechanicals' – effortfully rehearse a play to perform at Theseus' court. Unseen by them all except the bewitched weaver Bottom, the fairy king and queen Oberon and Titania play out their own marital struggle, involving and confusing the humans, while Oberon's attendant, Puck (the traditional country sprite Robin Goodfellow), creates mischief wherever he turns.

Shakespeare's well-designed plot is, unusually, largely his own, though the play borrows elements from Chaucer and Ovid. The lyrical language is close to that of *Romeo and Juliet*, and the plot of the mechanicals' play, *Pyramus and Thisbe*, is a comic rewriting of the tragedy's storyline. Aspects of the language are also similar to *Richard II*, and the three plays were probably written within a couple of years of each other.

MUCH ADO ABOUT NOTHING

1598-9

The progress of two parallel relationships forms the narrative of *Much Ado*. Beatrice and Benedick, one of the best known of Shakespeare's pairs of witty, argumentative lovers, start the play as verbal sparring partners but are tricked by their friends into acknowledging an underlying mutual love. Beatrice's cousin Hero, daughter of the governor of Messina, is wooed by Claudio, Benedick's friend, but in a darker trick, devised by the wicked Don John, is wrongly accused of infidelity. Claudio jilts her at the altar, she faints, and her friends declare her dead while her reputation is restored. This plot, widely popular in the Renaissance, was used a number of times by Shakespeare; it is reworked in the later tragicomedies and, in its most tragic form, in Othello.

Comic variation is provided by one of Shakespeare's great manglers of language, the constable Dogberry, and his companions, the headborough Verges and the Watch. These incompetent enforcers of the law in fact arrest the perpetrators of the plot against Hero, but are too stupid to realise the implications of their discovery.

Beatrice and Benedick have been popular with audiences and performers alike, providing effective partnership roles for a number of great actors.

First recorded performance: on 20 May 1613 John Heminges was paid £93. 6s. 8d. for a performance given at Whitehall as part of the celebrations for the wedding of Princess Elizabeth and the Elector Palatine.

OTHELLO

1603–4

Alone among Shakespeare's central tragedies, *Othello*, an intense and claustrophobic tale of marital and personal jealousies, is a domestic rather than a political or dynastic tragedy; its plot appropriately turns on a piece of personal linen, the heroine's dropped handkerchief.

Othello, a black general in the service of Venice, has wooed and won Desdemona, daughter of a Venetian senator. He angers his ensign Iago by appointing Cassio his lieutenant; Iago, jealous of Cassio and of Othello, with whom he suspects his own wife Emilia has been unfaithful, yearns for their destruction. Othello is sent to defend Cyprus against the Turks. Iago engineers the blame for a drunken brawl on to Cassio, and advises him to enlist Desdemona to plead his cause with Othello, while encouraging Othello to suspect Desdemona's infidelity with Cassio. Desdemona's handkerchief, Othello's gift, is dropped, surreptitiously taken and left in Cassio's room; when Othello asks Desdemona for it she cannot produce it. Enraged, Othello smothers Desdemona in her bedroom. Emilia enters and reveals the truth. Iago murders Emilia and flees. Othello kisses Desdemona and kills himself. Iago is apprehended and vows silence.

Writers including Shakespeare had previously presented black villains or comic characters, but Othello is unprecedented in western literature as a black tragic hero.

First recorded performance: on 1 November 1604, 'Hallamas Day', the King's Men performed 'A Play in the Banketinge house at Whit Hall Called The Moor of Venis', by 'Shaxberd'.

Undesirable characters

Shakespearean names to avoid

Old Gobbo	Abhorson	Snare
Peter Simple	Bullcalf	Sneak
Pompey Bum	Dogberry	Snout
Bottom	Bassett	Snug
Mouldy	Dull	Wart
Oatcake	Feeble	Lord Bigot
Potpan	Fang	Toby Belch
Sugarsop	Froth	Andrew Aguecheek

VI

'A Man of Fire‑new Words'

Shakespeare and Language

Shakespeare's longest word

Honorificabilitudinitatibus

Shakespeare did not actually invent this word, which appears at 5.1.40 in *Love's Labour's Lost*, a play in which he has fun with the elaborate styles and verbosity of the Elizabethan wordsmiths. *The Oxford English Dictionary* traces it back to Italy c. 1300 and finds several appearances of it or of similar versions of it around Shakespeare's time. Dr Johnson remarked that it was 'often mentioned as the longest word known'.

It means 'by honourableness' – and, luckily for actors trying to speak it, can be heard as a series of dactyls:

ho- | **no**-ri-fi- | **ca**-bi-li- | **tu**-di-ni- | **ta**-ti-bus

Soliloquy

Shakespeare has no heroes;
his scenes are occupied only with men.
Samuel Johnson, 1765

A lengthy speech by a character alone on the stage was fundamental to the technique of mid- and late-sixteenth-century drama — in the first instance often to cover costume changes. John Lyly, Christopher Marlowe, Thomas Kyd and Shakespeare were all particularly involved in its development.

The word *soliloquy* is first recorded by the *Oxford English Dictionary* in the 1613 edition of Robert Cawdrey's *Table Alphabetical*, where it is defined as 'priuate talke'. It became a definition for a 'literary production' representing such talk by the middle of the seventeenth century, when John Milton's use of it in this sense is the second example noted by the *OED*. The word arrived on the printed page, therefore, not long after the arrival of Shakespeare's *Hamlet* on the stage, at the turn of the century.

Characters alone on Shakespeare's stage in the early plays regularly address long speeches to the audience, generally explaining their motivation: the enormous role of Richard III contains energetic examples. It is not until *Hamlet*, however, that Shakespeare seems to arrive at the full potential of what we now think of as the soliloquy — a speech which feels as though it expresses the inward workings and complex progress of the thoughts of an individual. Such a speech may still contemplate an act, but it will seek to represent the fluctuating thought patterns and state of mind of the contemplater with a new subtlety. Shakespeare's growing mastery of the possibilities of the iambic pentameter, of compression and elliptical expression, enabled him to explore new levels of representation. The new awareness this suggests is part of the evidence put forward in proposing this period as the beginning of the modern concept of individual identity.

Blank verse

Blank verse – so called because of its unrhymed plainness – in its English form was devised in the late 1530s or early 1540s by Henry Howard, Earl of Surrey, as an appropriate form for his translation of Virgil's *Aeneid*. Surrey, an unreliable but gifted man born in 1517 and executed in 1547 by Henry VIII, was also an early exponent of the English sonnet.

Actors sometimes speak of iambic verse, with its regular, paired stressed and unstressed syllables, as being like a heartbeat.

Divided lines

Shakespeare sometimes divides a line of verse between two, three or even four speakers for 'realistic' and dramatic effect. Here Regan and her husband Cornwall bully the hapless Gloucester:

GLOUCESTER
   I have a letter guessingly set down
   Which came from one that's of a neutral heart,
   And not from one opposed.
CORNWALL   Cunning.
REGAN   And false.
                King Lear 3.7.47–9

King John and murderous Hubert conspiratorially divide a line into five:

KING JOHN
  Death.
HUBERT   My lord?
KING JOHN   A grave.
HUBERT   He shall not live.
KING JOHN   Enough.
               King John 3.2.76

And the Macbeths' nerves are shattered after Macbeth's murder of Duncan:

MACBETH
　　I have done the deed. – Didst thou not hear a noise?
LADY MACBETH
　　I heard the owl scream, and the crickets cry.
　　Did you not speak?
MACBETH　　　　　　When?
LADY MACBETH　　　　　　Now.
MACBETH　　　　　　　　　　As I descended?
LADY MACBETH
　　Ay.

Macbeth 2.2.14–17

How large was Shakespeare's vocabulary?

The number of distinct words in Shakespeare's work is just under 30,000; more usefully, the number of lexemes, or what we would think of as 'different' words, is under 20,000. This was an enormous vocabulary at the time – *Hamlet* has nearly twice as many different lexemes as, for example, Marlowe's *Doctor Faustus.*

By comparison, the lexeme vocabulary of an English-speaker today is likely to be between 30,000 and 50,000 words. Overall, the total number of English lexemes more or less doubled (to around 200,000) in the two centuries between about 1500 and 1700, a period of rapid growth. The number of words today is hugely larger (and harder to establish) in the scientifically complex modern world.

Rhetoric 3: Repetition

ANAPHORA

Anaphora, the repetition of the beginning of a phrase, is one of a number of repetition and patterning devices. It is a formalising device, lending gravitas and rhythmical weight. This highly rhetorical example, whose fame surely derives from its effective rhetoric as well as from its sentiment, also demonstrates **isocolon**, balancing phrases of the same length.

> This royal throne of kings, this sceptred isle,
> This earth of majesty, this seat of Mars,
> This other Eden, demi-paradise,
> This fortress built by Nature for herself
> Against infection and the hand of war,
> This happy breed of men, this little world,
> This precious stone set in the silver sea . . .
> This blessed plot, this earth, this realm, this England . . .
> *Richard II* 2.1.40–6, 50

EPIZEUXIS

Othello uses **epizeuxis**, the immediate repetition of a phrase, at the beginning of 5.2 when he enters Desdemona's bedchamber:

> It is the cause, it is the cause, my soul.

and again shortly afterwards:

> Put out the light, and then put out the light.

The effect is obsessive, troubled and uncomfortably ceremonial.

PLOCE

The similar **ploce** (pronounced 'plokey', meaning 'plaiting') is the repetition or interweaving of a word within the same phrase. It is used in *Romeo and Juliet* for youthful intensity:

> O Romeo, Romeo, wherefore art thou Romeo?

> Her I love now
> Did grace for grace and love for love allow.
> *Romeo and Juliet* 2.2.33, 2.3.81–2

EPISTROPHE

Intense again, and hypnotic, **epistrophe** is the repetition of a word at the end of clauses:

> Gaunt am I for the grave, gaunt as a grave.   *Richard II* 2.1.82

PERICLES
1607–8

This episodic tale was probably co-authored with the unsavoury George Wilkins, who wrote a novel on the same subject in 1608. The earlier sections are rambling and undeveloped in comparison with later episodes, where Pericles and his daughter Marina (whose name Shakespeare invented) are movingly reunited.

Pericles, Prince of Tyre, having angered King Antiochus, who has an incestuous relationship with his daughter, sets sail to escape Antiochus' revenge. On his travels he marries Thaisa, who apparently dies in childbirth and is thrown from Pericles' ship in a casket. Pericles leaves his daughter in the care of the governor of Tharsus, but she is sold off to a brothel by the governor's wife. Lysimachus, governor of Mytilene, is won by Marina's beauty and purity; Marina persuades the brothel-owner to retain her as a seamstress rather than a prostitute. Pericles arrives exhausted after long wanderings, and Marina's identity is revealed. They travel to Ephesus where they find Thaisa, who survived after all. The theme of the long-lost mother mirrors both the early *Comedy of Errors* and the late *Winter's Tale*.

Despite being omitted from the First Folio, perhaps because of its mixed authorship, *Pericles* was extremely popular for its first fifty years. Subsequently it sank into near oblivion, and it is still only rarely performed, though the later scenes and atmosphere of the sea can be very effective.

Early performance: the First Quarto (1609) announced its text 'As it hath been divers and sundry times acted by his Maiesties Servants, at the Globe on the Banck-side'.

Short and long words

The very markedly monosyllabic nature of Shakespeare's writing has long been noted. He is a master at using single-syllabled words for effect, and many of his verse lines are entirely monosyllabic. Hamlet's lines at 5.2.199–200 are a famous example of the use of short words. The effect of the long string of monosyllables is gnomic; and they slow the delivery and lead the ear to the single polysyllable 'readiness':

> If it be, 'tis not to come. If it be not to come, it will be now.
> If it be not now, yet it will come. The readiness is all.

The line 'To be, or not to be' works similarly (and comparison between the earlier and later versions (see pp. 90–1) makes clear the value of the final polysyllable). The first line of Mark Antony's oration on the death Julius Caesar (*Julius Caesar* 3.2.74) balances an orotund series of one, two and three syllables in the first half of the line with a second half consisting of four emphatic monosyllables:

> Friends, Romans, countrymen, lend me your ears.

The storm at the beginning of *King Lear* 3.2 needs no special effects other than Lear's language, which follows a hammered monosyllabic first line with rolling polysyllabic thunder, and slows again when he brings it all down on himself.

> Blow winds and crack your cheeks! Rage, blow!
> You cataracts and hurricanoes, spout
> Till you have drenched our steeples, drowned the cocks!
> You sulphurous and thought-executing fires,
> Vaunt-couriers of oak-cleaving thunderbolts,
> Singe my white head!

A little later in the same scene (68–9), Lear speaks in plain monosyllables to touching effect ('my self', now one word, was then more commonly two, as it is in the Folio).

> Come on, my boy. How dost my boy? Art cold?
> I am cold myself.

The lightly accented syllables of a long word may sound equally simple, and give a sense of intangible beauty. Cleopatra is 'A lass unparalleled', in a phrase where the liquid 'l's add to the effect (5.2.315), and the light 'i's and 'y's work a similar magic in *The Phoenix and Turtle* ('Let the bird of loudest lay') at 53–4:

> Beauty, truth and rarity,
> Grace in all simplicity.

New words

Writers of the late sixteenth and early seventeenth centuries are celebrated for their astonishingly creative linguistic inventiveness, and the list of words they came up with is exhilarating (a word first recorded as a description of marriage in John Milton's writings on divorce). Thousands of words and variants of words were invented at this time in the search for meaning and effect, and sent out to compete with one another in the jostling arena of new language. Some survived, many did not. The lasting fame of Shakespeare's plays has no doubt ensured that some of his coinages are still with us where those of others are not: contributions from Thomas Nashe, John Marston and Edmund Spenser were conspicuously less successful, and many fewer have survived. It remains the case that Shakespeare's inventiveness was outstanding.

Shakespeare constantly tried out words that he hadn't used before, and often invented new ones. In 1943 the scholar Alfred Hart reckoned that 170 words appear for the first time in written English, or are used with a new meaning, in *Hamlet* (our assessments of language use in this era can of course only be based on written texts). *Hamlet* is exceptional in the number of new usages, but not unique. Overall, David Crystal has reported, from a study of first recorded usages in *OED*, that Shakespeare is the first recorded user of 2,034 lexemes (excluding malapropisms and nonsense words). By comparison, he cites figures of around 800 for Thomas Nashe, 500 for Edmund

Spenser, 200 for the playwright John Marston and 50 for the King James Bible. Also high in Shakespeare is the proportion of new words to overall vocabulary: around 10%. The very early years of his career and the early 1600s, especially the years of writing the major tragedies, were points at which his linguistic invention reached its height.

Of his 2,034 new words, 357 are recorded by the *Oxford English Dictionary* as never being used again by anyone (at least in the sense used by Shakespeare); and over 900 eventually became obsolete. Many appear in the work of others in the years immediately following their appearance in his plays, and we have to assume that some of his 'new' words were in general use at the time. His total will therefore be somewhat less – Crystal suggests anywhere between 800 and 1,700. He notes that the *Oxford English Dictionary* gives Shakespeare as the first recorded user of 1,035 words where the next use is not recorded for at least 25 years – suggesting that Shakespeare's is indeed likely to have been the first use. The following selection is taken from those 1,035.

A selection of words first used by Shakespeare

accessible, acquired, acutely, affrighted, assembled, barefaced, batty, bedazzle, beguiling, bewitchment, blusterer, butchered, caged, cat-like, ceremoniously, cloud-capped, committed, compassion, comply, conquering, dawn, disturbed, dog-weary, droplet, (to) elbow, even-handed, eventful, flame-coloured, footfall, foul-mouthed, Frenchwoman, guiltily, hedge-pig, high-pitched, horridly, hostile, hot-blooded, hunchbacked, ill-starred, ill-used, inaudible, indistinguishable, insulting, irreconciled, laughable, leaky, leap-frog, marriage-bed, misquote, moonbeam, mortifying, neglected, neighbouring, newsmonger, night-owl, noiseless, obscenely, outsleep, outweigh, overpay, overpower, overrate, pageantry, pebbled, perusal, pleached, predecease, profitless, promising, prophetic, published, radiance, rat-catcher, raw-boned, reclusive, repeated, revealing, rose-cheeked, rose-lipped, sacrificial, satisfying, savagery, schooldays, sequestered, silliness, skirted, slippered, smirched, soiled, suffocating, suggesting, swans'-down, tardily, threateningly, three-legged, throw, time-honoured, useful, useless, ushering, well-behaved, well-bred, well-won

ROMEO AND JULIET

c. 1595–6

Romeo, a member of the Montague family of Verona, falls in love at first sight with fourteen-year-old Juliet Capulet, and she with him – but their two families are at odds. Romeo comes to her balcony at night and, with the connivance of Juliet's nurse, they agree to marry secretly. Immediately after their marriage, Romeo's friend Mercutio is killed in a street brawl, and Romeo, who has tried to stop the violence, kills Juliet's cousin Tybalt. He is banished from Verona. Juliet's parents plan to marry their daughter to the eligible Paris. In despair, Juliet takes a potion which apparently causes her death. The message telling Romeo the truth goes astray, and he poisons himself by her tomb. Waking too late from her drugged state, she finds his body, and stabs herself.

Shakespeare shaped a pre-existing story into the classic tale of young love and of youthful bravado and clan feuding. Critics over the years have complained at the reliance on coincidence and the setting of comic characters and vivid bawdiness alongside the central tragedy. But the conviction of the love story and the exuberant beauty of the play's language, brimming over with the newly fashionable sonnet form, overcome minor cavils.

Early performance: the first of its many performances was probably at the Theatre in Shoreditch.

Audiences in the seventeenth and eighteenth centuries found *Romeo and Juliet* too suggestive and inappropriately loaded with puns. David Garrick's adaptations of 1748 and 1750, which dominated the stage for the next hundred years, excised Romeo's first love for Rosaline, made Juliet an eighteen-year-old, removed puns and revised jaunty rhymes as more serious blank verse.

Playing with prefixes

One of the ways in which writers expanded the language was by experimenting with prefixes and suffixes. Spenser was fond of *-ful* (*groanful, sdeignful*), and Sidney of *well-* (*well-framed, well-liked, well-succeeding*). Shakespeare was keen on *a-* (*agoing*), *be-* (*besmirch*), *dis-* (*dislimb*), *out-* (*out-Herod*) and *re-* (*reword*). He was not alone in his enthusiasm for the innocuous-seeming prefix *un-*, but his enthusiasm for making creative use of it is very marked. The *Oxford English Dictionary* cites his as the first usage for 314 *un-* words, in a variety of adjectival, noun and adverbial forms. The majority of his *un-* words occur in plays written from 1600 on, and a third of his verb forms occur in four plays – *Richard II, Macbeth, Troilus and Cressida* and *Hamlet*. Macbeth offers us (as well as the new word *assassination*) six powerful examples whose quality seems to embody the dark destructiveness of the play.

unbend, unfix, unmake, unprovoke, unspeak, unsex

Rhetoric 4: Nouns become verbs

Shakespeare was particularly fond of **anthimeria** – turning nouns into verbs. The effect is energising:

Grace me no grace, nor uncle me no uncle.

Richard II 2.3.87

SIR THOMAS MORE

c. 1603–4

'The Book of Sir Thomas More' is a single, fragile manuscript containing a work which was never published or performed, but which is of great interest both because it includes manuscript copy probably by Shakespeare and because of the evidence it provides of collaborative composition. The first draft, mainly by Anthony Munday, was submitted to the censor, Edmund Tilney (see p. 51), sometime in the first half of the 1590s; he rejected it as it stood, chiefly because it showed insurrection by Londoners and insulted French immigrants. In 1603 further work was done on the manuscript, possibly because the death of Elizabeth I had made its content less sensitive. Several playwrights were involved, along with a theatre annotator, known to posterity as 'Hand C', who tidied it up for the stage. The text was emended throughout, and additional passages were interpolated in the manuscript where necessary.

The play follows the rise and fall of Thomas More, who becomes Henry VIII's Lord Chancellor but is beheaded for treason after refusing to accept the legitimacy of Henry's marriage to Anne Boleyn. It shies away from presenting the King, who never appears. Shakespeare's probable contribution consists of a passage of around 165 lines in which More puts down the 'Ill May Day' riot of 1517 by London citizens demonstrating against foreigners, and two other short passages.

An Englishman, an Irishman,
a Scotsman and a Welshman

The speech prefixes identifying the speaker at the beginning of each speech are sometimes revealing. In the Folio text of *Henry V* 3.2, which features an Englishman, an Irishman, a Scotsman and a Welshman among Henry's forces, Captain Fluellen is prefixed first by name but subsequently as *Welch.*, Captain Jamy is prefixed as *Scot.* and Captain Macmorris as *Irish*. The English captain Gower, however, always appears under his name.

These characters are chiefly identified, then, by their origin, and Shakespeare is carefully observant of their differing forms of speech. A number of non-standard spellings suggest pronunciation to the actor. Macmorris, for example, says 'be' for 'by' and 'beseeched' for 'besieged'. Fluellen has 'pody', 'plood' and 'prawls' for 'body', 'blood' and 'brawls', and 'aggriefed' and 'falorous' for 'aggrieved' and 'valorous', while Jamy's pronunciation is indicated in 'feith' and 'vary' ('very'). The pronunciations are carefully transcribed: the actor was not just asked to 'do' a regional accent.

Shakespeare also has fun with the French Princess Katherine's attempts at English and Henry's at French near the end of *Henry V*. And Edgar, reinforcing his disguise as beggar in the presence of the enemy in *King Lear*, adopts southern English forms and pronunciations such as 'ch'ill' for 'I'll' and 'vurther' for 'further' – forms that were even then largely obsolescent, and confined to the rural West Country, but were obviously already part of stock 'Mummerset'.

Vulgarity of language?

Shakespeare who many times has written better than any poet in any language is yet so far from writing wit always or expressing that wit according to the dignity of the subject that he writes in many places below the dullest writer of ours or any precedent age. Never did any author precipitate himself from such height of thought to so low expressions as he often does.

John Dryden, 1668

Rhetoric 5: Puns

Shakespeare's work is notoriously, even obsessively packed full of puns, so that we are aware of a constant alertness to potential meanings and implications. Hamlet is a compulsive punster, and his puns are part of the doubling and circling that pervades the play, and of his 'madness'. His first two lines contain intense, paradoxical and blatant puns (1.2.65, 67):

A little more than kin, and less than kind

and to his step-father, who remarks that 'the clouds still hang on you':

Not so much, my lord, I am too much in the 'son'.

Many of his puns are suggestive:

BRAKENBURY
With this, my lord, myself have naught to do.

RICHARD
Naught to do with Mistress Shore? I tell thee, fellow,
He that doth naught with her, excepting one,
Were best to do it secretly, alone.

Richard III 1.1.97–100

and so many of them are sexual double entrendres that whole books have been written about this subject alone.

Shakespeare is also fond of malapropism (the term postdates him), a device exemplified by Dogberry in *Much Ado About Nothing*: 'Comparisons are odorous', says the hapless constable – a similar mistake to Bottom's in *A Midsummer Night's Dream* (3.1), so perhaps it went down well the first time.

Stage directions 8: A cue to behaviour

Just occasionally, a striking direction is given for manner or behaviour:

The Cardinal in his passage, fixeth his eye on Buckingham, and Buckingham on him, both full of disdain.

Henry VIII 1.1.114

Enter Lear mad.   *King Lear* 4.6.80

Then comes dropping after all Apemantus discontentedly like himself.   *Timon of Athens* 1.2

❧ Sports and games ❧

Hunting and hawking

Most Tudor 'sports' were ultimately practice in skills used in battle, among them archery (which Henry VIII had obliged ordinary subjects to practise regularly) and the often dangerous sport of hunting. Hunting and hawking are regular occupations of the nobility in the plays. Hawking provides an extended metaphor for Petruccio's taming of Katherina (4.1.179–200).

Fig. 12. Queen Elizabeth at a hunting picnic, from George Turberville, *The Noble Art of Venerie*, 1575.

Tennis

Real or royal tennis was the sport of kings and lords – under Henry VIII it had been restricted by law to the upper classes. It features in *Henry V*: the Dauphin of France sends Henry a 'treasure' – a set of tennis balls – and the sport becomes a metaphor for war between the countries. Tennis balls were stuffed with hair, as old balls (stuffed with dog's hair) found at Whitehall and Westminster Hall have proved; when Benedick has been to smarten himself up at the barber's in preparation for his wooing of Beatrice, Claudio quips that 'the old ornament of his cheek hath already stuffed tennis balls' (*Much Ado About Nothing* 3.2.42–3).

Chess

Miranda and Ferdinand are discovered by Prospero playing chess (*The Tempest* 5.1.171). It was an aristocratic game, suitably decorous for young unmarried people, and a mirror of the serious 'game' of courtly love. It features frequently in romance tales and on wedding-chests and mirror-cases. A few other passing wordplays on queens, bishops, checks and so on suggest Shakespeare's familiarity with the game, and that he knew his audience would understand them.

Football

Football, on the other hand, was a plebeian game. Kent calls Goneril's steward Oswald a 'base football player' in *King Lear* (1.4.84–5). It was described by Sir Thomas Elyot in *The Governor* (1531) as a game of 'beastly fury and extreme violence'.

Nine-men's-morris

This age-old game was played in ancient Egypt, Greece, Troy and Rome, as well as in the Far East, and is still played as a board game and even online. It was very popular in medieval England, not only with the laity but also with monks. Boards cut into cloister seats or at the foot of columns – as at Chester cathedral, for example – can still be seen today. It involved moving pegs, or 'men' to outwit your opponent, and could also be played outdoors on a 'board' cut into turf. The outdoor, village version is mentioned in *A Midsummer Night's Dream* (2.1.98), where the fairy queen Titania complains that the pitch is filled up with mud, a symptom of the disorder caused by the rift with her partner Oberon.

How to play nine-men's-morris

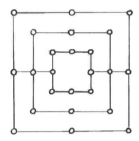

For two players

Nine-men's-morris board

Eighteen pieces or men in two colours, nine of each

The players agree who will start the first round. There are no pieces on the board at the start of the game.

The players take it in turns to place one of their pieces on an unoccupied circle. When a player manages to place three pieces in a 'mill', or linked row (i.e. this must be a vertical or horizontal row, not a diagonal), they may remove one of their opponent's pieces from the board and from play. An opponent's piece may only be removed from a mill if no other piece is available.

When all the pieces have been placed on the board, the players take it in turns to move their own pieces in an attempt to form new mills. In each turn a player moves a single piece, which may be moved only one space, along the lines linking the circles. A piece may only be moved on to an empty space – it cannot jump over an opponent's piece or knock it off the board. When a mill is formed, an opponent's piece may be removed. If one move creates two mills, two of the opponent's pieces may be removed. A player must make a move when it is their turn.

When one player cannot move, or has only two pieces left on the board and is unable to form a mill, their opponent has won the game.

THE TAMING OF THE SHREW

1590–5?

In an Induction to the play proper, Christopher Sly, a drunken tinker, is persuaded by an aristocratic hunting party that he is a lord who has not been in his right mind for fifteen years. They put on an entertainment for him.

Baptista Minola of Padua has two daughters, the outwardly compliant Bianca and the shrewish Katherina. Bianca has three suitors, two of whom disguise themselves as tutors. Petruccio hears of Katherina's vast dowry and despite her protests offers to marry her. He arrives for the wedding in fantastic rags (see p. 104), an opening move in what turns into an uncomfortably entertaining taming strategy. One of Bianca's suitors transfers his attentions to a wealthy widow, and she secretly agrees to marry another. The marriage is revealed, and at their wedding the three bridegrooms bet twenty crowns on who has the most obedient wife. The three women are summoned, but only Katherina appears. She makes a long speech in praise of wifely duty.

The controversial ending allows directors various interpretations of Petruccio's scheme: that it is straightforwardly successful, or abusive, or leads both characters to maturity. Whatever ending is chosen, the play's hugely enjoyable energy has made it enduringly popular on stage and screen.

Rhetoric 6: Word tennis

Richard III has a fine example of **stichomythia**, the alternation of lines or part lines between characters, in a scene in which Richard woos the newly widowed Anne (1.2.195–205). It is a formal device from classical drama, but still extremely effective in conveying aggression and pressure and, in this case, sexual tension.

ANNE
  I would I knew thy heart.

RICHARD
  'Tis figured in my tongue.

ANNE
  I fear me both are false.

RICHARD
  Then never man was true.

ANNE
  Well, well, put up your sword.

RICHARD
  Say then my peace is made.

ANNE
  That shalt thou know hereafter.

RICHARD
  But shall I live in hope?

ANNE
  All men I hope live so.

RICHARD
  Vouchsafe to wear this ring.

ANNE
  To take is not to give.

It is equally effective when used for banter in *Love's Labour's Lost* (2.1.181–92), or earnest lovers' discourse in *A Midsummer Night's Dream* (1.1.136–40).

Stichomythia produces a similar tension when Hamlet confronts his mother (3.4.8–11), where the tension is heightened further by Hamlet's angry and mocking use of **epistrophe**, the ending of lines or phrases with the same words. Gertrude's use of 'thou' and Hamlet's formal, dutiful and distancing 'you' are also striking.

QUEEN
Hamlet, thou hast thy father much offended.

HAMLET
Mother, you have my father much offended.

QUEEN
Come, come, you answer with an idle tongue.

HAMLET
Go, go, you question with a wicked tongue.

Flap-dragon

We get a flavour of domestic jollity in *Love's Labour's Lost* (5.1.40–1): 'thou art easier swallowed than a flap-dragon.' A flap-dragon or snap-dragon is a raisin set alight in brandy or a similar spirit, and swallowed by the daring. This sport survived to become a popular parlour-game in the nineteenth and even early twentieth centuries; it features in Charles Dickens's *Pickwick Papers* and is what Lewis Carroll is referring to with his snap-dragon-fly in *Through the Looking-Glass*: 'Its body is made of plum pudding, its wings of holly-leaves, and its head is a raisin burning in brandy.'

Ten compliments

Age cannot wither her, nor custom stale
Her infinite variety.
Antony and Cleopatra 2.2.245–6

Think you there was or might be such a man
As this I dreamt of?
Antony and Cleopatra 5.2.92–3

A lass unparalleled.
Antony and Cleopatra 5.2.315

Heavenly Rosalind!
As You Like It 1.2.278

I could have better spared a better man.
1 Henry IV 5.4.103

In thy face I see
The map of honour, truth and loyalty.
2 Henry VI 3.1.202–3

This was the noblest Roman of them all.
Julius Caesar 5.5.69

A maid
That paragons description.
Othello 2.1.61–2

He hath a daily beauty in his life.
Othello 5.1.19

O, she doth teach the torches to burn bright.
It seems she hangs upon the cheek of night
As a rich jewel in an Ethiop's ear –
Beauty too rich for use, for earth too dear.
Romeo and Juliet 1.5.44–7

Ten insults

I do desire we may be better strangers.
As You Like It 3.2.251

These tedious old fools.
Hamlet 2.2.214

The devil damn thee black, thou cream-faced loon!
Macbeth 5.3.11

Thou lily-livered boy . . . What soldiers, whey-face?
Macbeth 5.3.15, 17

You Banbury cheese!
The Merry Wives of Windsor 1.1.120

KATHERINA   Asses are made to bear, and so are you.
PETRUCCIO   Women are made to bear, and so are you.
The Taming of the Shrew 2.1.200–1

A whoreson beetle-headed, flap-eared knave.
The Taming of the Shrew 4.1.143

Thou flea, thou nit, thou winter-cricket, thou!
The Taming of the Shrew 4.3.111

Thou debauched fish, thou.
The Tempest 3.2.25–6

He has not so much brain as ear-wax.
Troilus and Cressida 5.1.51–2

THE TEMPEST

1610–11

Alonso, King of Naples, his son Ferdinand and his ally Antonio, Duke of Milan, are shipwrecked on an island in a storm conjured by Prospero, exiled brother of the usurper Antonio. Prospero lives on the island with his daughter, Miranda, the spirit Ariel, and the original inhabitant, the savage Caliban. Miranda and Ferdinand meet and fall in love. Prospero's magic and Ariel's music confuse the castaways, including drunken members of the ship's crew. Eventually the characters all meet. Miranda, who has never seen a human being apart from her father, is astonished at the beauty of mankind; Prospero forgives Antonio, reveals that the fleet is unharmed, and releases Ariel. Caliban is dispatched to tidy Prospero's cell.

The Tempest is the first play in the First Folio, and the last play of which Shakespeare was sole author. Unusually for him, the plot observes the dramatic unities. Like *A Midsummer Night's Dream*, the play is one of a handful whose plot was his own, and the atmosphere of magic harks back to the earlier play, while Prospero and Ariel are reminiscent of Oberon and Puck. The material, though, seems to have been inspired by several recent publications.

First recorded performance: 1 November 1611, Hallowmas Day, the King's Men for James I at Whitehall.

Sources for *The Tempest*, all dated 1610

William Strachey, 'A True Reportary of the Wracke and Redemption of Sir Thomas Gates', a manuscript from Virginia.

Silvester Jourdan, *A Discovery of the Burmudas, otherwise called the Ile of Divels.*

Council of Virginia, *A True Declaration of the Estate of the Colonie in Virginia* .

Shakespeare was acquainted with a number of people involved in the Virginia Company, including the Earls of Pembroke and Southampton. Strachey's report, full of the language of wonder and amazement, is paralleled strikingly in the play. Ariel's account of his electric activities in the storm (1.2.196–206), for example, recalls Strachey's description:

Onely upon the thursday night Sir George Summers being upon the watch, had an apparition of a little round light, like a faint Starre, trembling, and streaming along with a sparkeling blaze, halfe the height upon the Maine Mast, and shooting sometimes from Shroud to Shroud . . . running sometimes upon the Maine-yard to the very end, and then returning.

VII

'Our Thoughts Are Ours, Their Ends None of Our Own'

Afterlife

Rewriting Shakespeare

The Bowdlers and the Lambs

Seventeenth/ and eighteenth/century adapters and editors often changed the plays to suit contemporary taste. In a long/lived late/seventeenth/century version of *King Lear* by Nahum Tate, Lear survives to live out his days in peace, and Cordelia and Edgar, happily married, rule Britain. Dr Johnson famously found Cordelia's death in the original so distressing that he could scarcely bear to contemplate reading the last scenes of the play again.

Nahum Tate
describes King Lear *in 1680*

A heap of jewels, unstrung and unpolished; yet so dazzling in their disorder, that I soon perceived I had seized a treasure.

Adapters and producers were not alone in finding aspects of Shake/speare's work vulgar, indecent or too painful. Shakespeare had been writing for playgoing Elizabethans and Jacobeans, but over time, as he became a monument of national literature, these elements became ever more problematic for a domestic readership. Among others, two brother/and/sister teams, the Bowdlers and the Lambs, looked for solutions.

'Out, crimson spot!'

THOMAS AND HENRIETTA BOWDLER

Henrietta Bowdler (1750–1830) and her brother Dr Thomas Bowdler (1754–1825), like many children from educated families in their day, were read the works of Shakespeare by their parents in their early years – chiefly by their father, who carefully omitted passages he considered unsuitable for the childish mind. This proved a lifelong inspiration. In 1807 Henrietta published the *Family Shakespeare* – twenty plays in four volumes, from which she had excised crude or doubtfully suggestive passages. 'It will, I believe,' she affirmed in her preface, 'be universally acknowledged, that few authors are so instructive as Shakespeare; but his warmest admirers must confess, that his Plays contain much that is vulgar, and much that is indelicate.' This first, anonymous publication (it would not have been thought a respectable project for a woman) was not successful, but her brother, who had devoted much of his life to prison reform, took up the task in retirement and in 1818 issued a full collection of the plays in ten volumes. This time the project succeeded, and frequent reprints followed over the next few decades.

The eponymous term 'to bowdlerise' remembers the Bowdlers appropriately, since it was a shared family activity. Their mother had published, in 1775, an exhortatory commentary on an expurgated edition of the Song of Solomon, and Thomas himself also undertook the lengthy task of cleaning up Gibbon's *Decline and Fall of the Roman Empire*. The popular view is that the Bowdlers provided euphemistic and therefore ludicrous substitutes for Shakespeare's indelicate phrases, but examples of this are in fact few, and their chief activity was cutting 'only those words and expressions which cannot with propriety be read aloud in a family'. History has not been kind to them, and 'to bowdlerise' became a term of ridicule within twenty years of publication. Their work was widely popular, however, in the nineteenth century, and no doubt many parents were grateful for it.

The Victorian poet Algernon Swinburne wrote: 'More nauseous and foolish cant was never chattered than that which would deride the memory or depreciate the merits of Bowdler. No man ever did better service to Shakespeare than the man who made it possible to put him into the hands of intelligent and imaginative children.'

TIMON OF ATHENS

1604–5?

Coleridge described *Timon of Athens* as an 'after vibration' or 'still-born twin' of *King Lear*, with which it shares themes and vocabulary. Around a third of the play, however, is probably by Middleton. It has never been a popular play – but Timon does not require us to like him.

The play falls into two parts. Timon, a rich Athenian, revels in being generous to artists, friends and servants, despite cynical comments from the philosopher Apemantus. But after a lavish banquet rumours circulate that his money is all gone, and he is pursued by creditors; his friends are evasive when asked for help. Timon invites them to dinner once again. Thinking that his fortunes are restored, they accept, but he offers them dishes containing stones, and drives them out, vowing misanthropy.

Retreating to the woods, followed only by his faithful servant Flavius, Timon digs for roots but finds gold, which he gives away to prostitutes and thieves. He refuses to help defend Athens against Alcibiades, another disgruntled self-exile. He writes his own epitaph, and at his death is buried on the seashore.

The play is notable for having inspired Karl Marx, who drew on it to argue that money alienates individuals from their personal capabilities and therefore from themselves.

'To teach courtesy, benignity, generosity, humanity . . .
easy reading for very young children'

CHARLES AND MARY LAMB

Charles Lamb (1775–1834), best known as an essayist, was the son of a lawyer's clerk in London. He became a friend of the poet Samuel Taylor Coleridge while at school, and later of other young writers with an interest in political reform, including Percy Bysshe Shelley and the essayist William Hazlitt. His life, however, was not easy. A speech impediment hindered him from taking up the kind of career he might otherwise have hoped for, and the family lost their livelihood when the father's employer died. Both Charles and his sister Mary (1764–1847) suffered from mental illness. Charles endured serious depression, while in 1796 Mary, 'worn down to a state of extreme nervous misery by attention to needlework by day and to her mother at night', in a fit of mania stabbed and killed her very difficult mother with a table knife. Supported by friends, Charles managed to save her from lifelong imprisonment by undertaking to care for her himself.

Despite all these trials, in 1807 – the same year that Henrietta Bowdler produced her first *Family Shakespeare* – the Lambs published *Tales from Shakespeare*, a beautifully written and imaginative retelling for children of twenty of the plays, using as much of Shakespeare's language as possible. In particular, the book was intended for girls as well as boys, as they noted in their preface: 'because boys being generally permitted the use of their fathers' libraries at a much earlier age than girls are, they frequently have the best scenes of Shakespeare by heart, before their sisters are permitted to look into this manly book'. The *Tales* were deservedly popular, and have never since been out of print.

Charles Lamb

writing in 1811 and aware how harsh life can be,
was distressed at the inhumanity revealed in King Lear

To see Lear acted – to see an old man tottering about the stage, turned out of doors by his daughters in a rainy night, has nothing in it but what is painful and disgusting.

TITUS ANDRONICUS

1590–4

The plot of this early and gory play is, unusually, original. Titus, a Roman, is pitted against Tamora, Queen of the Goths and wife of Saturninus, the new Emperor of Rome, and her black servant and lover, Aaron. Amidst the jockeying for power and revenge, Titus' daughter Lavinia is raped at Aaron's instigation by Tamora's sons, who cut out her tongue and lop off her hands to prevent her revealing them as her attackers. Titus' sons are accused of the crime; he agrees to have his hand cut off to save them from death, but Aaron has them killed nonetheless. Upon discovering the truth, Titus murders Tamora's sons and serves them up in a pie to Tamora and Saturninus; he kills Lavinia and Tamora and is killed by Saturninus who, in turn, is killed by Titus' son Lucius, who becomes emperor.

Titus Andronicus (possibly co-authored with George Peele) is a revenge tragedy in the popular mode of the 1580s and 1590s. Nonetheless, in its subtle and questioning presentation of the values of Romans and Goths it looks forward to the ambiguities of *Antony and Cleopatra* and *Coriolanus*. Hugely successful when it first appeared, it later fell out of favour, considered uneven in quality and unacceptably violent. Renewed interest in the late twentieth century showed it to be theatrically highly effective, and it has appealed equally to audiences and critics.

First recorded performance: 24 January 1594, by Sussex's Men, at the Rose, recorded in Henslowe's diary as 'titus & ondronicus', earning £3. 8s. – it was already financially a very successful play.

A single copy of a 1594 Quarto edition of *Titus Andronicus* surfaced in Sweden in 1904. This is the earliest known printing of any of Shakespeare's plays.

The Pre-Raphaelites' list of Immortals

Painting Shakespeare

Representation of Shakespeare's works in art has a long history, including distinguished works by William Hogarth, William Blake and Henry Fuseli, as well as many illustrations, and enjoyed particular popularity in the paintings of the Pre-Raphaelites. The Pre-Raphaelite Brotherhood, founded in 1848 by John Everett Millais and his friends William Holman Hunt, a fellow-student at the Royal Academy of Arts, and Dante Gabriel Rossetti, aimed to approach painting with a close attention to nature, and 'to sympathise with what is direct and serious and heartfelt in previous art', an aim which took them back to painting before the time of the 'academic' Raphael. The group also had strong literary inclinations, and published a journal entitled *The Germ*.

Among their declarations of belief was a 'list of Immortals, forming our creed' – the two 'first-class' members of this list being Jesus and Shakepeare. In the brief years of the group's existence they produced a number of paintings of Shakespearean scenes. The best-known is probably Millais' *Ophelia* (1851–2), which like many of their works depicts a young woman with long hair, here floating round her in the brook. Millais (in 1851) and Rossetti (later, in 1870) both portrayed Mariana, from Tennyson's poem inspired by *Measure for Measure*, and Holman Hunt painted several Shakespearean scenes, including *Claudio and Isabella* (1850–3) and *Valentine Rescuing Sylvia from Proteus* (1851).

Despite acquiring additional members, the Brotherhood was short-lived, and was more or less defunct by 1853. Its influence on ideas and painting style had nonetheless been considerable, and interest in medievalism, literary subjects and Shakespeare in particular, persisted through the rest of the nineteenth century.

Divine Shakespeare?

Laurence Olivier thought Shakespeare 'the nearest thing in incarnation to the eye of God'.

TROILUS AND CRESSIDA

1601–2

Shakespeare's disillusioned tale of the Trojan War, which in its own era had a chequered publication and performance history, has come into its own in the twentieth century and its aftermath. It reworks the plot of *Troilus and Criseyde*, subordinating Chaucer's story of love and faithlessness to the depiction of an aimless war characterised by bickering, braggadocio, backbiting, betrayal and unheroic death.

Troilus woos Cressida with the enthusiastic aid of her uncle Pandarus. They declare their love, but she is handed over to the Greeks in a prisoner exchange and, somewhat reluctantly, transfers her affections to her Greek escort, Diomedes. Meanwhile the Trojans debate the merits of keeping Helen, and Ulysses and the other Greek leaders argue amongst themselves, observed by the scurrilous and cynical Thersites, who summarises the world of the play as 'wars and lechery'. The play ends in battle: Troilus bests Diomedes, Achilles is finally roused to fight, but is driven back by Hector. As it grows dark, Hector unarms, and is killed by Achilles' Myrmidons; his body is dragged round the battlefield tied to Achilles' horse.

This ambiguous play is described in the 1609 Quarto as a 'Famous History' and a comedy; in the First Folio, however, it appears among the tragedies. Early performance is uncertain. One version of the 1609 Quarto edition proclaims that the play has been acted at the Globe, another describes it as 'never staled with the stage, never clapper-clawed with the palms of the vulgar'.

John Dryden, adapting the play in 1679, rather took the edge off the traditional plot by making Cressida faithful to Troilus throughout.

Shakespeare in music

Shakespeare must have been fond of music. It is used throughout his work, in directions for alarms, sennets and offstage music, and many songs. In addition, it is often heard at moments of deep and quiet feeling, as, for example, in the 'magical' coming to life of Hermione in *The Winter's Tale*, and as accompaniment to Lorenzo's speech to Jessica in the last act of *The Merchant of Venice*. Those who have no music in themselves (like Cassius, the conspirator against Julius Caesar, who 'hears no music') are, as Lorenzo says, not to be trusted.

A baker's dozen of the innumerable musical works inspired by Shakespeare

A Midsummer Night's Dream (overture)	Mendelssohn, 1826
The Tempest (fantasy overture)	Berlioz, 1830
King Lear (overture)	Berlioz, 1831
Roméo et Juliette (choral symphony)	Berlioz, 1839
Hamlet (symphonic poem)	Liszt, 1858
Romeo and Juliet (fantasy overture)	Tchaikovsky, 1869
The Tempest (symphonic phantasy)	Tchaikovsky, 1873
Hamlet (overture and incidental music)	Tchaikovsky, 1888
Falstaff (symphonic study)	Elgar, 1913
The Tempest (incidental music, suites)	Sibelius, 1925
Romeo and Juliet (ballet)	Prokofiev, 1935–6
Serenade to Music (for 16 voices and orchestra, from *The Merchant of Venice*)	Vaughan Williams, 1938
A Midsummer Night's Dream (incidental music)	Carl Orff, 1952

TWELFTH NIGHT

1601

A combination of wit, broad comedy, underlying melancholy and beauty of language has made *Twelfth Night* one of Shakespeare's best-loved comedies. The intertwined plots centre round the household of Olivia, a countess in mourning for her brother. Two twins, brother and sister, have been shipwrecked off the coast of Illyria. Viola, believing her brother Sebastian to have drowned, enters the service of Duke Orsino disguised as a page-boy, Cesario. On his behalf she pays court to Olivia but, awkwardly, Olivia falls for the beautiful young servant instead of the master, while Viola herself has fallen in love with Orsino. Olivia's cheerful cousin Sir Toby Belch and his companion Sir Andrew Aguecheek join forces with her waiting-woman Maria to get their own back on Olivia's sanctimonious steward Malvolio by convincing him that Olivia has fallen for him. Thoroughly misled, he dresses up in yellow cross-gartered stockings to please her. Feste the clown comments with biting wit on all the goings-on. Olivia transfers her affections to Sebastian, who is not lost after all, confusing him with Cesario. All is finally revealed. Viola and Sebastian are movingly reunited, and Viola can finally admit her secret love for Orsino. Malvolio, like Shylock, is left uncomfortably humiliated and unrevenged.

First recorded performance: 2 February 1602, Candlemas Day, in the Middle Temple Hall, a performance noted by the law student John Manningham in his diary, where he highlighted the trick played on Malvolio. The early popularity of the subplot is also apparent in the play's revival at court in 1623 under the title 'Malvolio'.

Opera

Since Matthew Locke's incidental music written for Dryden and Davenant's version of *The Tempest* in 1667, the plays of Shakespeare have provided an inspiration and an irresistible challenge to composers for the stage. Operas setting them to music number nearly 300. Few, however, are often performed, and only Verdi's *Otello* and *Falstaff* feature among the most popular of all operas. Some remain more faithful to Shakespeare than others: Britten's *A Midsummer Night's Dream* uses Shakespeare's text only, apart from a single brief inserted line sung in a rapid monotone. Verdi's *Macbeth,* on the other hand, offers Lady Macbeth as the main character and a large chorus of Witches. Rossini's *Otello* of 1816 avoids the suggestively intimate handkerchief, and features instead a more conventionally tasteful mysterious letter – though he was bold enough to finish the opera with an onstage murder.

PLAYS MOST FREQUENTLY SET AS OPERAS

The Tempest
A Midsummer Night's Dream
Hamlet
Twelfth Night
Romeo and Juliet

PLAYS NEVER (OR NOT YET) SET AS OPERAS

1, 2, 3 Henry VI
King John
Richard II
Titus Andronicus

NINE SHAKESPEARE OPERAS WORTH HEARING

The Fairy Queen (*A Midsummer Night's Dream*)
Henry Purcell, 1692

Macbeth
Giuseppe Verdi, 1847

Die lustigen Weiber von Windsor (*The Merry Wives of Windsor*)
Otto Nicolai, 1849

Béatrice et Bénédict (*Much Ado About Nothing*)
Hector Berlioz, 1862

Roméo et Juliette
Charles Gounod, 1867

Otello
Giuseppe Verdi, 1887

Falstaff (*The Merry Wives of Windsor*)
Giuseppe Verdi, 1893

Sir John in Love (*The Merry Wives of Windsor*)
Ralph Vaughan Williams, 1929

A Midsummer Night's Dream
Benjamin Britten, 1960

ONE DERIVED FROM SHAKESPEARE NOT TO BE MISSED

Lady Macbeth of Mtsensk (via a short story by Nikolai Leskov)
Dmitri Shostakovich, 1934

AN INTERESTING FAILURE

Das Liebesverbot (*Measure for Measure*)
Richard Wagner, 1836

AND A COUPLE THAT GOT AWAY:
GREAT OPERAS THAT WERE NEVER WRITTEN

The Tempest – a possible next opera by Mozart, though
he died before plans got very far

King Lear – first projected by Verdi in 1843, and a plan he kept
returning to but never fulfilled, although he lived until 1901

Musicals

Shakespeare's popularity, plots and stagecraft were equally a draw from the early days to writers of musicals. The first half of the twentieth century saw *The Belle of Mayfair* (*Romeo and Juliet*), by Leslie Stuart (1906), and more famously, *The Boys from Syracuse* (*The Comedy of Errors*), by Richard Rodgers and Lorenz Hart (1938). By far the two best-known musicals are Cole Porter's *Kiss Me, Kate* (*The Taming of the Shrew*, 1948), and *West Side Story* (*Romeo and Juliet*), by Leonard Bernstein and Stephen Sondheim (1957).

Henry Irving

after hearing his voice recorded onto one of Edison's wax cylinders

You speak into it and everything is recorded, voice, tone, intonation, everything. You turn a little wheel, and forth it comes, and can be repeated ten thousand times. Only fancy what this suggests. Wouldn't you like to have heard the voice of Shakespeare, or Jesus Christ?

Shakespeare in film

In 1899 the actor Sir Herbert Beerbohm Tree produced a short film – probably an advertisement for a stage version – showing sequences from *King John*. The four-minute deathbed scene that survives is the first known Shakespeare on film; it was also distributed in card form designed for '*What The Butler Saw*' kinetoscope machines. A number of other, longer films were made during the silent era. The earliest full-length sound film of a Shakespeare play was *The Taming of the Shrew*, starring Douglas Fairbanks and Mary Pickford, in 1929. It was followed by, among others, *A Midsummer Night's Dream* (1935), with a cast including James Cagney, Mickey Rooney and Olivia de Havilland, and George Cukor's *Romeo and Juliet* (1936), with Norma Shearer, Leslie Howard and John Barrymore. The first British feature-length film was Paul Czinner's *As You Like It* (1936), notable also for starring the young Laurence Olivier as Orlando, and for its score by William Walton. More recent British films have included versions by

Kenneth Branagh of *Henry V* (1989), *Much Ado About Nothing* (1993) and his epic four-hour *Hamlet* (1996).

There are well over 400 feature-length filmed versions or adaptations of Shakespeare's works, and by far the most-filmed plays are *Romeo and Juliet* (77) and Hamlet (75).

A DOZEN BEST FILMS

Henry V	Laurence Olivier, 1944
Hamlet	Laurence Olivier, 1948
Richard III	Laurence Olivier, 1955
Throne of Blood (*Macbeth*)	Akiro Kurosawa, 1957
Hamlet	Grigori Kosintsev, 1964
Chimes at Midnight (*1, 2 Henry IV*)	Orson Welles, 1965
Romeo and Juliet	Franco Zeffirelli, 1968
Macbeth	Roman Polanski, 1971
Ran (*King Lear*)	Akiro Kurosawa, 1985
Richard III	Richard Loncraine, 1996
William Shakespeare's Romeo + Juliet	Baz Luhrmann, 1996
10 Things I Hate About You (*The Taming of the Shrew*)	Gil Junger, 1999

THE MOST ENJOYABLE FILM ABOUT SHAKESPEARE

Shakespeare in Love   John Madden, 1998

SEVEN GREAT FILM SCORES

Henry V	William Walton, 1943–4
Hamlet	William Walton, 1947
Macbeth	Jacques Ibert, 1948
Julius Caesar	Miklós Rósza, 1953
Richard III	William Walton, 1955
Hamlet	Dmitri Shostakovich, 1964
King Lear	Dmitri Shostakovich, 1969

What the dickens

Everyday phrases

Many of our everyday phrases are found in Shakespeare's plays. Some of them were in common use in his own time, and many featured in collections of *sententiae*, pithy proverbs, which he would have studied at school. Others have become part of the language because they are his. Examples are innumerable – they include:

All's Well That Ends Well
The title

Antony and Cleopatra
it beggared all description (2.2.208)

As You Like It
that was laid on with a trowel (1.2.102)
thereby hangs a tale (2.7.28)
we have seen better days (2.7.121)
can one desire too much of a good thing? (4.1.113–14)
it is meat and drink to me (5.1.11)
an ill-favoured thing . . . but mine own (5.4.57–8)

The Comedy of Errors
the why and the wherefore
neither rhyme nor reason (both 2.2.48)

Cymbeline
the game is up (3.3.107)
I have not slept one wink (3.4.100)

Hamlet
more in sorrow than in anger (1.2.230)
brevity is the soul of wit (2.2.90)
hoist with his own petard (3.4.205)
a ministering angel (5.1.230)

1 Henry IV
set my teeth . . . on edge (3.1.127)
the better part of valour is discretion (5.4.118–19)

Henry V
stiffen the sinews (3.1.7)

2 Henry VI
smooth runs the water where the brook is deep (3.1.53)
as dead as a doornail (4.10.39)

Julius Caesar
it was Greek to me (1.2.283)

Macbeth
the be-all and the end-all (1.7.5)
what's done is done (3.2.12)
at one fell swoop (4.3.219)

The Merchant of Venice
with bated breath (1.3.122)
truth will out (2.2.77)
all that glisters is not gold (2.7.65)
a Daniel come to judgement (4.1.221)
pound of flesh (several times)

The Merry Wives of Windsor
what the dickens (3.2.17)

A Midsummer Night's Dream
fancy-free (2.1.164)

Much Ado About Nothing
as merry as the day is long (2.1.42–3)
good men and true (3.3.1)

Othello
wear my heart upon my sleeve (1.1.63)
the green-eyed monster (3.3.168)
pomp and circumstance (3.3.357)
a foregone conclusion (3.3.430)

Richard III
short shrift (3.4.94)
dance attendance (3.7.55)
a tower of strength (5.3.12)

The Taming of the Shrew
the more fool you (5.2.135)

The Tempest
a sea-change (1.2.401)

Troilus and Cressida
good riddance (2.1.117)

Twelfth Night
midsummer madness (3.4.56)

Eminent Shakespeareans

Actors

THOMAS BETTERTON
(1635–1710)
Hamlet, Timon, King Lear, Falstaff, Angelo, Othello

DAVID GARRICK
(1717–79)
Richard III, Hamlet, Macbeth, Benedick, Romeo, Leontes

JOHN PHILIP KEMBLE
(1757–1823)
Hamlet, Richard III, Shylock, Othello, Macbeth,
Lear, Antony, Prospero, Iago, Wolsey

EDMUND KEAN
(1789–1833)
Shylock, Richard III, Hamlet, Othello, Timon,
Coriolanus, Wolsey, King John

WILLIAM CHARLES MACREADY
(1793–1873)
Macbeth, King Lear, Coriolanus, Cassius, Hubert,
Wolsey, Prospero, Shylock, Leontes

EDWIN BOOTH
(1833–93)
Richard III, Hamlet, Othello/Iago (with Henry Irving)

HENRY IRVING
(1838–1905)
Hamlet, Shylock, Othello/Iago, Benedick,
Malvolio, Wolsey

FRANK BENSON
(1858–1939)
Hamlet, Coriolanus, Richard II, King Lear, Petruccio

JOHN BARRYMORE
(1882–1942)
Hamlet, Richard III

PAUL ROBESON
(1898–1976)
Othello

[188]

JOHN GIELGUD
(1904–2000)
Hamlet, Prospero, Richard II, Romeo/Mercutio (with Olivier)

LAURENCE OLIVIER
(1907–89)
Richard III, Macbeth, Hamlet, Henry V, Hotspur,
Shylock, Romeo/Mercutio, Titus Andronicus, Coriolanus

MICHAEL REDGRAVE
(1908–85)
Bolingbroke, Berowne, Macbeth, Hamlet, King Lear,
Richard II, Antony, Prospero

ORSON WELLES
(1915–85)
Falstaff, King Lear, Othello, Macbeth

John Wilkes Booth assassinates Abraham Lincoln

John Wilkes Booth (1839–65) was a member of a successful acting family.
His father, Junius Brutus Booth, had left England for the United States
where he became famous for his portrayal of Richard III. His brother Edwin,
the finest actor of the family, enjoyed a highly successful career playing
major Shakespearean roles in the United States and Britain. John Wilkes, a
strikingly handsome and athletic man, played a variety of Shakespearean
characters, including Hamlet and Richard III, but said that his favourite role
was Brutus, 'the slayer of a tyrant'.

Unlike his brother, John Wilkes was strongly pro-Confederate and anti-
Abolitionist, and with two collaborators he plotted the assassination of
President Lincoln, Vice-President Andrew Johnson and Secretary of State
William H. Seward (the other two planned assassinations failed). On 14 April
1865 the President attended Ford's Theatre in Washington. Earlier in the
day Booth had bored a spy-hole in the door of the President's box; that
evening, entering the box during the performance, he shot Lincoln in the
back of the head. He leaped from the box onto the stage and cried 'Sic
semper tyrannis' ('Thus ever to tyrants', the motto of Virginia and a phrase
attributed to Brutus), before making his escape. He was tracked down to a
farm in Virginia, surrounded in a tobacco barn and shot in the neck.

In the late nineteenth century *Julius Caesar* became the first Shakespeare
play to feature in the secondary school curriculum in the USA. It was a
suitable choice: the curriculum was still based on Latin, Greek and classical
studies; students were mostly male, and the play is mainly (safely) about
men; and it teaches a good lesson – that it's not wise to assassinate a ruler.

PAUL SCOFIELD
(1922–2008)
Mercutio, Don Armado, Henry V, Troilus, Hamlet,
Coriolanus, King Lear

RICHARD PASCO
(b. 1926)
Richard II/Bolingbroke (with Ian Richardson), Orsino, Jaques

CHRISTOPHER PLUMMER
(b. 1929)
Henry V, Hamlet, Leontes, Mercutio, Macbeth,
Mark Antony, Richard III, Benedick, Iago

IAN RICHARDSON
(1934–2007)
Pericles, Iachimo, Richard II/Bolingbroke

BRIAN BEDFORD
(b. 1935)
Ariel, Angelo, Orlando, Timon

ALAN HOWARD
(b. 1937)
Richard II, Richard III, Henry V, Henry VI,
Theseus/Oberon, Coriolanus, King Lear

DEREK JACOBI
(b. 1938)
Hamlet, Benedick, Claudius, Malvolio, King Lear

IAN MCKELLEN
(b. 1939)
Richard II, Macbeth, Iago, Coriolanus, Richard III

MICHAEL GAMBON
(b. 1940)
Othello, Coriolanus, King Lear, Antony, Falstaff

AL PACINO
(b. 1940)
Richard III, Shylock

MICHAEL PENNINGTON
(b. 1943)
Angelo, Berowne, Hamlet, Henry V, Richard II

ANTONY SHER
(b. 1949)
Richard III, Malvolio, Shylock, Leontes, Macbeth, Iago

KENNETH BRANAGH
(b. 1960)
Benedick, Hamlet, Richard III, Henry V, Iago

MARK RYLANCE
(b. 1960)
Hamlet, Romeo, Benedick, Olivia, Cleopatra

SIMON RUSSELL BEALE
(b. 1961)
Ferdinand, Thersites, Richard III, Ariel, Malvolio,
Benedick, Julius Caesar, Macbeth, Leontes, Hamlet

Actresses

SARAH SIDDONS
(1755–1831)
Isabella, Constance, Desdemona, Ophelia, Katherine,
Cleopatra, Volumnia, Lady Macbeth

SARAH BERNHARDT
(1844–1923)
Cordelia, Desdemona, Hamlet

ELLEN TERRY
(1847–1928)
Duke of York, Mamillius, Puck, Prince Arthur,
Fleance, Titania, Desdemona, Ophelia, Portia,
Lady Macbeth, Cordelia, Volumnia

ADA REHAN
(1859–1916)
Rosalind, Katherine, Viola

CONSTANCE BENSON
(1860–1946)
Lady Anne, Lady Macbeth, Katherina

SYBIL THORNDIKE
(1882–1926)
Queen Katherine, Volumnia, Constance, Lady Macbeth,
Queen Margaret, Mistress Quickly

EDITH EVANS
(1888–1976)
Nurse, Rosalind, Queen Katherine

PEGGY ASHCROFT
(1907–91)
Desdemona (with Paul Robeson), Juliet, Beatrice,
Viola, Rosalind, Cleopatra, Queen Margaret

DOROTHY TUTIN
(1931–2001)
Viola, Juliet, Ophelia, Portia, Rosalind,
Cressida, Queen Katherine

JUDI DENCH
(b. 1934)
Juliet, Ophelia, Viola, Imogen, Beatrice, Regan,
Lady Macbeth, Cleopatra, Volumnia

VANESSA REDGRAVE
(b. 1937)
Rosalind, Katherine, Imogen, Cleopatra, Prospero

HELEN MIRREN
(b. 1945)
Cleopatra, Cressida, Diana, Hero, Ophelia,
Isabella, Queen Margaret

SINÉAD CUSACK
(b. 1948)
Beatrice, Celia, Lady Macbeth, Katherine, Portia

HARRIET WALTER
(b. 1950)
Helena, Imogen, Viola, Cleopatra

KATHRYN HUNTER
(b. 1956)
King Lear, Cleopatra, The Fool (*King Lear*)

JULIET STEVENSON
(b. 1956)
Isabella, Cressida, Rosalind

FIONA SHAW
(b. 1958)
Celia, Katherine, Richard II

THE TWO GENTLEMEN OF VERONA

1590–4

Valentine is sent to Milan to broaden his experience of life; there he falls in love with Silvia. His friend Proteus follows him, with his servant Lance and Lance's dog Crab, leaving his beloved, Julia, behind. Proteus also falls in love with Silvia, and reveals to her father that she and Valentine plan to elope. Valentine is banished; he and his servant Speed are captured by outlaws, who offer him the choice between death and becoming their leader. Julia arrives disguised, enters Proteus' employment, and woos Silvia on his behalf. Silvia follows Valentine, and Proteus follows her, eventually attempting rape. When he repents, Valentine offers to yield him Silvia, but Julia faints, and her identity is revealed. Proteus repents further, and the 'correct' relationships are restored.

Probably Shakespeare's first comedy, this play, though scrappily plotted and uncomfortable in its denouement, is enjoyable and occasionally eloquent. Lance's prose monologues concerning Crab are a highlight. Julia is the first of his roles for boy actors playing women dressed as men. Like Viola in *Twelfth Night*, she becomes a servant to the man she loves: the name she takes is Sebastian, that of Viola's twin brother. However, Shakespeare never again attempted a comic dog.

THE TWO NOBLE KINSMEN

c. 1613–14

Written with John Fletcher, this play probably represents Shakespeare's final contribution to the stage. It may well have been the first work staged at the swiftly rebuilt Globe after its destruction by fire in 1613. Its complex language and highly formal scenes – alternating with low comedy involving the Jailer's Daughter and a group of morris dancers – may suggest, though, along with its lavish use of music, that its authors conceived it as a Blackfriars play.

The story (derived from Chaucer's 'Knight's Tale') concerns two cousins, Palamon and Arcite, who fall in love with the same woman. After the fall of Thebes they have been imprisoned by Theseus, and catch sight of Emilia from their prison window. Arcite is freed and banished, but returns in disguise. The Jailer's Daughter falls in love with Palamon and organises his escape. While she searches vainly for him in the forest and loses her wits, the cousins begin a duel. They are interrupted by Theseus, who decrees that they shall fight for Emilia formally in a month's time; the loser must die. Emilia cannot decide which man she prefers. Arcite wins the contest, but before Palamon can be executed Arcite is killed falling from his horse; he bequeathes Emilia to his cousin.

THE WINTER'S TALE

'A sad tale's best for winter': this tale of death and regeneration, losing and finding, moves from tragedy to comedy as though in seasonal renewal. It is told in language at one moment difficult, beautiful and formal, and at the next fluently comic.

Leontes, jealous to the point of insanity, accuses his wife Hermione of infidelity with his friend Polixenes, and loses his son and apparently also his wife. Antigonus secretly saves their newborn daughter, but is killed by a bear. The figure of Time divides the play, ushering in a second part infused with spring and new life. Leontes' daughter Perdita has been brought up by a shepherd in Polixenes' Bohemia. At a rustic sheep-shearing feast Perdita distributes flowers, and Polixenes' son Florizel declares his love for her. They escape his father's wrath by fleeing to Leontes' court, where Perdita's identity is revealed. Perdita and Leontes are moved when Paulina shows the company a lifelike statue of Hermione. Paulina calls for music and the statue is revealed as the living Hermione.

To a basically borrowed romance plot Shakespeare added Paulina, his own invention and a figure of great moral weight, and the restoration of Hermione. The contrasting figure of the pedlar Autolycus takes his roguery from pamphlets about the London underworld.

First recorded performance: 11 May 1611, at the Globe, recorded by Simon Forman; he was particularly struck by Autolycus, who proved an enduringly popular character.

The play's two-part structure was intolerable to eighteenth-century taste. David Garrick devised a successful version which removed the first three acts and made the play a comedy about love triumphing over social distinctions. And it was an eighteenth-century editor, Thomas Hanmer, who tactfully corrected Shakespeare's apparent error in referring to the (non-existent) coast of Bohemia by altering the location to Bithynia throughout.

A Chronology
of Shakespeare's Plays

The exact dates of composition of the plays in which Shakespeare was involved will never be certain. Estimates of the order in which they were written are made on the basis of a combination of evidence from contemporary records of performance and publication of the texts; the few references in the plays to external events; and stylistic development and choice of subject.

Shakespeare's earliest plays, written before the Chamberlain's Men were formed in 1594, probably include:

1589—94

1589—91	*1, 2, 3 Henry VI*
1590—5?	*The Taming of the Shrew*
1590—4	*The Two Gentlemen of Verona*
1590—4	*Titus Andronicus* (with George Peele?)
c. 1591—3	*Richard III*
c. 1592—4	(*Edward III*)
c. 1594	or earlier, *The Comedy of Errors*

The Chamberlain's Men played at the Theatre from 1594 until the opening of the Globe theatre in 1599, during which time Shakespeare probably wrote:

1594—99

c. 1594—5	*Love's Labour's Lost*
c. 1594—6	*A Midsummer Night's Dream*
c. 1595	*Richard II*
c. 1595—6	*Romeo and Juliet*
c. 1590—6	*King John*
1596—7	*The Merchant of Venice*
1596—7	*1 Henry IV*

1597–8   *2 Henry IV*
1597   *The Merry Wives of Windsor*
1598–9   *Much Ado About Nothing*

The opening of the Globe in 1599 must have provided both inspiration and a commercial imperative. In that year, too, the writing of English histories (and of topical satire) was strictly limited under the Bishops' Ban, because of anxieties about the succession and possible rebellion or assassination. Between then and the death of Queen Elizabeth in spring 1603 may be dated:

1599–1603

1599   *Henry V*
1599   *Julius Caesar*
c. 1599–1600   *As You Like It*
c. 1600   *Hamlet*
1601   *Twelfth Night*
1601–2   *Troilus and Cressida*
c. 1602–5   *All's Well That Ends Well*

From around 1603, Shakespeare seems to have worked at a slightly less hectic rate:

1603–8

1603–4   *Othello*
c. 1604   *Measure for Measure*
1603–4   *(Sir Thomas More)*
1604–5?   *Timon of Athens*
1604–6   *King Lear*
c. 1606   *Macbeth*
c. 1606   *Antony and Cleopatra*
1607–8   *Pericles*
c. 1608   *Coriolanus*

After 1608/9 the company was able to make use of the indoor and in some ways more sophisticated Blackfriars playhouse. Between then and 1614 Shakespeare worked on six final plays, the last three written in collaboration with John Fletcher.

1609–14

HISTORICAL EVENTS

1558 Death of Queen Mary, accession of Elizabeth I

1559 Acts of Supremacy and Uniformity restore an Anglican Church independent of Rome

1564 Plague in Stratford

1566 James VI of Scotland born

1570 Queen Elizabeth excommunicated by Pope Pius V

1575 Queen Elizabeth spends two weeks at Kenilworth Castle, Warwickshire, entertained by the Earl of Leicester

1580 Francis Drake completes circumnavigation of the world

1585 First (unsuccessful) English colony in North America established by Sir Walter Ralegh in Virginia

1586 Star Chamber decrees restrict printing to the City of London and one press each at Oxford and Cambridge; famine year

1587 Mary, Queen of Scots executed

1588 Failure of the Spanish Armada

1594 Four-year famine begins

1597 Poor Law introduces taxation and establishes 'working houses' to relieve the poor

1599 Earl of Essex fails to put down Irish Rebellion

1601 8 February, Essex rebellion; 25 February, Essex executed; Earl of Southampton imprisoned in the Tower of London

1603 Death of Elizabeth I and accession of James I and VI of Scotland; Sir Walter Ralegh condemned for treason

1605 Gunpowder plot

1607 Jamestown, first successful English colony in North America, established

1611 The King James Authorised Version of the Bible published

A Biographical Chronology

Many dates are approximate

	LIFE	RELATED EVENTS	WORKS
1564	Born around 21–23 April, christened 26 April in Stratford-upon-Avon	Plague in Stratford-upon-Avon	
1566	Gilbert (brother) born		
1568	Father serves as town bailiff (to 1569)	Richard Burbage born	
1569	Joan (sister) born	Queen's Men and Worcester's Men are the first professional acting companies to play in Stratford	
1571	Anne (sister) born; father chief alderman and justice of the peace; WS eligible for entry to Stratford Grammar School		
1572		Ben Jonson born; Leicester's Men play at Stratford	
1573		Henry Wriothesley, 3rd Earl of Southampton, born	
1574	Richard (brother) born	Warwick's and Worcester's Men play at Stratford	

1576	The Theatre opens	
1577	The Curtain opens	
1578	Strange's and Essex's Men play at Stratford Anne (sister) dies; WS leaves school by now, probably earlier	
1579	John Fletcher born	
1580	William Herbert, 3rd Earl of Pembroke born; Berkeley's Men play at Stratford Edmund (brother) born	
1581	Worcester's Men play at Stratford	
1582	Berkeley's Men play at Stratford WS marries Anne Hathaway late 1582	
1583	Queen's Men formed Daughter Susanna born (christened in May)	
1585	Twins Hamnet and Judith born	
1586	Death of Sir Philip Sidney	
1587	The Rose opens; several companies, including the Queen's Men, play at Stratford Father forced to leave Corporation of Stratford	
1589	Thomas Kyd's *Spanish Tragedy*	
1590	Philip Sidney's *Arcadia* and Edmund Spenser's *Faerie Queene* 1–3 published	
1591	Philip Sidney's *Astrophil and Stella* published	Over this period writes *1, 2, 3 Henry VI* *The Taming of the Shrew* *The Two Gentlemen of Verona* *Titus Andronicus, Richard III,* *(Edward III), Comedy of Errors*

	LIFE	RELATED EVENTS	WORKS
1592	First (rivalrous) reference to WS in print, in *Greene's Groats-worth of Wit*; John Shakespeare listed as a recusant	Plague in London; *Greene's Groats-worth of Wit* published; death of Greene; Henslowe starts diary	
1593		Death of Christopher Marlowe; plague year, theatres closed	Publishes *Venus and Adonis* and *Titus Andronicus*; writes early sonnets?
1594		Chamberlain's Men formed; plague year, theatres closed; *Comedy of Errors* performed at Gray's Inn	Publishes *The Rape of Lucrece*
1595	Recorded as a member of the recently formed Chamberlain's Men, and as performing before the Queen	The Swan opens	Over this period writes *Love's Labour's Lost* *A Midsummer Night's Dream* *Richard II* *Romeo and Juliet*
1596	Death of son Hamnet; applies for coat of arms for his father	Complete *Faerie Queene* (1–6) published	*King John* *1 Henry IV*
1597	Buys New Place, one of the largest houses in Stratford; listed as tax defaulter in the parish of St Helen's, Bishopsgate in London	Theatres briefly closed after *The Isle of Dogs* causes scandal at the Swan	*The Merchant of Venice* *2 Henry IV* *The Merry Wives of Windsor*
1598	Name first appears on the title-pages of his plays – quartos of *Richard II*, *Richard III* and *Love's Labour's Lost*	The Theatre dismantled	*Much Ado About Nothing*
1599		Death of Edmund Spenser; the Globe theatre built and opened	*Henry V*, *Julius Caesar* *As You Like It*

1600	The Fortune opens	*Hamlet*
1601	John Shakespeare (father) dies	*Twelfth Night* *Troilus and Cressida*
1602	Essex's supporters commission performance of *Richard II*	*All's Well That Ends Well*
1603	WS plays leading role in Ben Jonson's *Sejanus*	Death of Elizabeth in March, theatres closed for mourning; James I becomes patron of renamed King's Men, 19 May; plague 1603–4, theatres closed	*Othello* *Measure for Measure* (*Sir Thomas More*)
1604		Plague; King's Men take part in James's coronation procession	*Timon of Athens* *King Lear*
1605	Buys tithes in Stratford		
1606	Susanna (daughter) fined for refusing to receive communion at Easter		*Macbeth* *Antony and Cleopatra*
1607	Susanna marries John Hall; Edmund (brother), a player, dies in London	Theatres closed for three months	*Pericles*
1608	Mary Shakespeare (mother) dies; first grandchild, Elizabeth Hall, born	Lease on Blackfriars theatre reverts to Richard Burbage; plague in London 1608–10	*Coriolanus*
1609	Spends more time in Stratford from now on	Plague	[Publication of sonnets, dedicated to Mr. W.H.] *The Winter's Tale*
1610		Ben Jonson's *The Alchemist*	*Cymbeline* *The Tempest*
1611	Contributes to legal costs of a Highways Bill		

LIFE	RELATED EVENTS	WORKS
		Henry VIII
		(*Cardenio*)
		The Two Noble Kinsmen
1612 Gilbert (brother) dies		
1613 Buys London property; Richard (brother) dies	Globe theatre burns down during performance of *All is True* (*Henry VIII*) on 29 June; the Hope opens	
1614	Rebuilt Globe opens	
1616 WS dictates first draft of will, January; Judith (daughter) marries Thomas Quiney, 10 February; WS revises will, 25 March; dies, 23 April in Stratford; grandson Shakespeare Quiney born November		
1619	Richard Burbage dies	
1623	Publication of the First Folio	

Works Consulted and Recommended Reading

Editions: complete works

The Arden Shakespeare Complete Works, gen. eds Richard Proudfoot, Ann Thompson and David Scott Kastan, 2nd edn, London, 2001

The Complete Works of Shakespeare, ed. David Bevington, 4th edn, New York, 1992

The First Folio of Shakespeare, the Norton Facsimile, ed. Charlton Hinman, with an introduction by Peter Blayney, 2nd edn, New York and London, 1996

The Riverside Shakespeare, ed. G Blakemore Evans *et al.*, 2nd edn, Boston and New York, 1997

William Shakespeare: The Complete Works (Oxford Shakespeare), ed. Stanley Wells, Gary Taylor, John Jowett and William Montgomery, 2nd edn, Oxford, 2005

William Shakespeare: The Complete Works (The Pelican Shakespeare), ed. Alfred Harbage, Harmondsworth, 1969

Editions: individual plays

The Arden Shakespeare, gen. eds Richard Proudfoot, Ann Thompson, David Scott Kastan and Henry Woudhuysen

The New Cambridge Shakespeare, gen. eds A.R. Braunmuller and Brian Gibbons

The Oxford Shakespeare, gen. eds Stanley Wells and Gary Taylor

The Penguin Shakespeare, gen. ed. Stanley Wells

Biographical

Jonathan Bate, *The Genius of Shakespeare*, London, 1997

Katherine Duncan-Jones, *Shakespeare: An Ungentle Life*, London, 2010

Park Honan, *Shakespeare: A Life*, Oxford, 1998

E.A.J. Honigmann, *Shakespeare: The 'Lost Years'*, Manchester, 1985, rev. edn 1988

Samuel Schoenbaum, *Shakespeare's Lives*, New York, 1970

——————, *William Shakespeare: A Documentary Life*, New York, 1975

James Shapiro, *1599: A Year in the Life of William Shakespeare*, London, 2005

Stanley Wells, *Shakespeare: A Dramatic Life*, London, 1994

Players and theatres

Gerald Eades Bentley, *The Profession of Dramatist in Shakespeare's Time 1590–1642*, Princeton, 1971

————, *The Profession of Player in Shakespeare's Time 1590–1642*, Princeton, N.J., 1984

Andrew Gurr, *Playgoing in Shakespeare's London*, Cambridge, 1987, 3rd edn 2004

————, *The Shakespearian Playing Companies*, Oxford, 1996

Scott McMillin and Sally-Beth MacLean, *The Queen's Men and their Plays*, Cambridge, 1998

David Wiles, *Shakespeare's Clown: Actor and Text in the Elizabethan Playhouse*, Cambridge, 1987

Language

David Crystal, *The Stories of English*, London, 2004

———— and Ben Crystal, *Shakespeare's Words: A Glossary and Language Companion*, London 2002

E.A.J. Honigmann, *The Texts of 'Othello' and Shakespearian Revision*, London, 1996

Frank Kermode, *Shakespeare's Language*, London and New York, 2000

Eric Partridge, *Shakespeare's Bawdy*, London, 1947, 3rd edn 1968

Stanley Wells and Gary Taylor, *William Shakespeare: A Textual Companion*, Oxford, 1987

Reference and general

The Compact Edition of the Oxford English Dictionary, Oxford, 1971

David Crystal and Ben Crystal, *The Shakespeare Miscellany*, London, 2005 (particularly for language)

David Hugh Farmer, *The Oxford Dictionary of Saints*, Oxford, 1978, 2nd edn 1987

Halliwell's Film, Video and DVD Guide, ed. John Walker, 23rd edn, London, 2008

The New Kobbé's Opera Book, ed. Earl of Harewood, and Antony Peattie, London, 1997

New Oxford Companion to Music, ed. Denis Arnold, Oxford, 1983

The Oxford Companion to Shakespeare, ed. Michael Dobson and Stanley Wells, Oxford, 2001

Oxford Dictionary of Art, ed. Ian Chilvers, Harold Osborne and Dennis Farr, Oxford, rev. edn 1997

Marvin Spevack, *A Complete and Systematic Concordance to the Works of Shakespeare*, vols 1–3, Hildesheim, 1968

Further reading

Peter Ackroyd, *Shakespeare: The Biography*, London, 2005

Claire Asquith, *Shadowplay: The Hidden Beliefs and Coded Politics of William Shakespeare*, New York, 2005 (arguing for a Catholic Shakespeare)

Jonathan Bate, *Soul of the Age: The Life, Mind and World of William Shakespeare*, London, 2008

Anthony Burgess, *A Dead Man in Deptford*, London, 1993 (on Marlowe)

——, *Nothing Like the Sun: A Story of Shakespeare's Love-life*, reissue, New York, 1996 (an investigation in novel form of Shakespeare's attitude to love)

——, *Shakespeare*, London, 1970

Eamon Duffy, *The Stripping of the Altars: Traditional Religion in England, 1400–1580*, New Haven and London, 1992

Stephen Greenblatt, *Will in the World: How Shakespeare Became Shakespeare*, London and New York, 2004

Anthony Holden, *William Shakespeare: The Man Behind the Genius*, Boston, 1999

Ted Hughes, *Shakespeare and the Goddess of Complete Being*, London, 1992

Charles and Mary Lamb, *Tales from Shakespeare*, ed. Marina Warner, London, 2007

Peter Levi, *The Life and Times of William Shakespeare*, London, 1988

Charles Nicholl, *The Reckoning*, London, 1992, 2nd edn 2002 (on Marlowe)

James Shapiro, *Contested Will: Who Wrote Shakespeare?*, New York and London, 2010

Index of Play Synopses